LETTERS ON THE ATONEMENT

By the
Rev. Richard Treffry, Jun.

Author of
Treatise on Christian Perfection

"We joy in God through our Lord Jesus Christ, by whom we have now received the atonement." —ROMANS v. 11.

SCHMUL PUBLISHING COMPANY
NICHOLASVILLE, KENTUCKY

COPYRIGHT © 2021 BY SCHMUL PUBLISHING CO.
All rights reserved. No part of this publication may be reproduced or used in any form or by any means—graphic, electronic, or mechanical, including photocopying, recording, taping, or information storage or retrieval systems—without prior written permission of the publishers.

Churches and other noncommercial interests may reproduce portions of this book without prior written permission of the publisher, provided such quotations are not offered for sale—or other compensation in any form—whether alone or as part of another publication, and provided that the text does not exceed 500 words or five percent of the entire book, whichever is less, and does not include material quoted from another publisher. When reproducing text from this book, the following credit line must be included: "From *Letters on the Atonement* by Richard Treffry, Jr., © 2021 by Schmul Publishing Co., Nicholasville, Kentucky. Used by permission."

    This Schmul Publishing Co. edition is not a scanned facsimile of a used book. It has not been "updated" or edited into modern English, punctuation or grammar, but is accurate to the author's own style and usage. The text has been carefully proofread for accuracy and formatted for easier reading by today's readers. Every effort has been made to prevent disordered text.

Cover image copyright: <a href="https://www.123rf.com/profile_cdrewunser">cdrewunser / 123RF Stock Photo</a>. Used by permission.

Published by Schmul Publishing Co.
PO Box 776
Nicholasville, KY 40340
USA

ISBN 10: 0-88019-635-1
ISBN 13: 978-0-88019-635-2

Visit us on the Internet at www.wesleyanbooks.com, or order direct from the publisher by calling 800-772-6657, or by writing to the above address.

Contents

Publisher's Preface/**5**

Letter I/**8**

Letter II/**14**

Letter III/**23**

Letter IV/**35**

Letter V/**48**

Letter VI/**58**

Letter VII/**70**

Letter VIII/**80**

Letter IX/**88**

Letter X/**97**

Letter XI/**113**

Letter XII/**124**

Letter XIII/**136**

Letter XIV/**148**

Letter XV/**157**

Letter XVI/**170**

Publisher's Preface

THE SPIRITUAL ASSAULT OF the great Adversary has moved beyond attacking Christian practices to undermining the foundational beliefs of the Church. It was not so long ago that believers, not only holiness people, were sneered at for avoiding alcohol, tobacco, movies, dancing and immodest dress. Now, darkness is creeping farther in from the edges as some theologians, scholars and clergy— yes, even some Wesleyans— voice doubt about cardinal doctrines such as hell and the atonement.

These are not new propositions or innovative ideas. Apostates have been around for centuries. What is alarming is the hearing they are now receiving in the Church world, including in some Wesleyan circles.

Richard Treffry, Jr., addressed several such deviations from truth in his day, and the book now before you is a carefully reasoned defense of the doctrine of the atonement. Hebrews 12:2 says we should be "Looking unto Jesus the author and finisher of our faith; who for the joy that was set before him endured the cross, despising the shame, and is set down at the right hand of the throne of God." A contemporary with

Treffry, Adam Clarke forcefully and beautifully asserted in his commentary on this verse that Jesus, by

> "fulfilling the will of the Father... in tasting death for every man; and having endured the cross and despised the shame of this ignominious death, He is set down at the right hand of God, ever appearing in the presence of God for us, and continuing his exhibition of himself as our Sacrifice, and his intercession as our Mediator."

What a glorious comfort and hope!

In *Letters on the Atonement*, Treffry directs a loving plea to one who is teetering on the edge of heresy. His in-depth reasoning is considered, sound and authentically scriptural. It is also (unfortunately) appropriate for our day. Jesus warned that false teachers will arise in the Church, and every generation must be on guard against their toxic doctrines. The saints have affirmed the truth of Christ's atoning sacrifice since the days of the apostles. It remains a bedrock belief for the Faithful.

—D. Curtis Hale
Publisher

Letters on the Atonement

Letter I.

My dear Friend,

It is with much regret I learn that you are troubled with doubts upon the subject of the atonement of Christ, and other points of the Socinian controversy. Yet let me not be supposed to intimate, that I esteem such matters improper subjects for investigation, or that I imagine their truth will be rendered at all questionable by the most severe and rigid inquiry. I am so far from this, that I should sincerely rejoice (were it practicable) for every believer in the New Testament to make himself fully acquainted with the points at issue between us and the Unitarians: nor can I for a moment doubt, that an unprejudiced survey of the arguments on both sides, would lead to a maturity and establishment of faith not usual in the present condition of the Christian church.

While I believe that the Bible is a revelation from God, I cannot, however, conceal from myself,—and I would fain impress it affectionately upon you,—that the doctrines of Scripture are not to be understood and appreciated independently of certain moral and spiritual qualifications; and that these are only to be secured by a devout, sincere, and believing application to the throne of grace. To the natural man, whose mind is entirely without the enlightening influence of divine grace, the spiritual revelations of the evangelic system are foolishness. Being discerned only by spiritual senses, he who is destitute of such a power of perception remains in a state of ignorance of, or aversion from them, deep and dense in the proportion in which his mind is destitute of divine and heavenly light. Yet, "if any man lack wisdom," he is encouraged to "ask it of God," with the assurance, derived from the divine character, and confirmed by the experience of all ages, that "He giveth to all liberally, and upbraideth not."

Such being the condition on which divine illumination is made to depend, I cannot but feel concerned to find that you are at all disposed to waver upon the doctrine of the atonement of Christ, because, in the nature of things, your doubts must exert some degree of influence upon the spirit in which you approach God, to seek for the assistance which you need. Of this I find you are already sensible. In adverting to your past feelings, you will recollect that you came to the duty of prayer with a strong and delightful confidence. You felt humbly assured that you might successfully plead the merit and intercession of Christ, not only in seeking pardon for sin, but also in petitioning for any spiritual good, of your need of which you were sensible. Nor were your prayers without success. You will remember how delightfully your faith in Christ was confirmed; how frequently you were enabled to realize views of divine truth, which were at once surprising and refreshing to your spirit; and how sweetly you were strengthened to pursue a course of humble obedience to the will of God. But this is past. You have not, I trust, abandoned the duty of secret prayer; but your approach to God is no longer marked by the confidence which once distinguished it; you are embarrassed in the presence of Him to whom it was once your delight to draw near. You no longer feel the prevalency of the name and the virtue of the blood of Christ, as you once enjoyed them. Duty and suffering are comparatively irksome; and of your closet and your home it may well be said, "The glory is departed."

There is something in your circumstances indescribably affecting to my mind; and that, not merely because you are already a sufferer, but also because your position is at present so extremely critical. You are not, I believe, yet the subject of that pernicious latitudinarianism which represents every system of belief as equally acceptable to God, provided it be not accompanied by any gross outrage of morality. You are still ready to admit, that Christianity is not only the best form of religion, but also that there is no other by which you can attain the enjoyment of eternal happiness. But suffer me, my dear friend, to remind you, that, in all essentials, there is but one Christianity. He who rejects the doctrine of the atonement, and he who believes in it, cannot both be Christians. They have, in fact, no community. He who worships Christ as God, and he who represents him as "fallible and peccable man," cannot be partakers of the same religion: both, it is true, believe that there is a God; but they are essentially at issue as to who and what God is. If we be right, the Unitarian is a blasphemer: if we be wrong, we are idolaters. There is no alternative, there can be no alternative. Nothing, therefore, can be more serious than your present circumstances; and any decisive change in your opinions will obviously involve consequences more momentous than you are at present able to calculate. I need not, then, urge upon you the necessity of deep deliberation, of solemn concern, of earnest prayer.

But suffer me to suggest to you the reproach which your conduct will cast upon those whom you so deeply love, should you unhappily take that step to which your doubts at present tend. You have enjoyed the communion of saints, and with deep reverence have you looked up to those Christians of mature and ripened piety, with whom it has been your happiness to be associated. Of some of them you have thought almost as you would think of angels of God. Their simple faith, their earnest zeal, their pure benevolence, their strict integrity, their gentleness and spirituality, have conspired to impress you with so exalted a view of Christianity, that you have wondered how any could resist its attractions. Some of them you have visited in their last hours, and your tears even now are ready to start, when you recur to the scenes of more than mortal peace which you then witnessed, of "joy unspeakable, and full of glory;" the triumph over death, and all its associated terrors; the resignation of those best loved into the hands of God; the clear, cloudless anticipation of eternal blessedness. It is impossible that you can ever forget how resolutely you determined, "This people shall be my people, their God shall be my God." But continue to cherish the doubts which now agitate you, till they are matured into certainty, and till you feel yourself bound to renounce all connexion with those who have hitherto been your choicest associates, and you, in effect, declare to the world, that all this peace, virtue, and joy, is mere delusion; that the ground of that hope, which has waxed more vigorous and bright in sorrow and in death, is a mere fable; and that ninety-nine out of a hundred of those called "Christians" are gross idolaters.

I do not wish to appeal to your feelings at the expense of your judgment. No; look fairly at the case, and tell me, is this conclusion likely to be true? Is it at all probable, that all that Christian experience which is founded on the doctrine of the atonement of Christ should be a dream? Is it to be believed, that the lives and deaths of men dishonouring God in the most gross manner, should be thus peaceful, heavenly, triumphant? Can you for an instant suppose, that the great body of the church, so called, is allowed to fall into deadly heresy? and that multitudes, countless multitudes, die not only without repentance, but triumphing above everything else in their most pestilential error? Are you able to bring yourself to the conclusion, that a good and gracious God would permit a multitude of sincere men, men remarkable for the humbleness of their minds, to continue to dishonour his government, by giving his glory to another; and to pass into eternity unrepentant and unforgiven? Your heart revolts from such a conclusion; and yet this is the conclusion to which you must come, if you reject the atonement, and, of consequence, the divinity of Christ.

But perhaps you will reply, that the Unitarian does not believe that the worshippers of Jesus will be punished in a future life, for their errors while in this world. Perhaps not, but it must be on the supposition that idolatry is not sin, or, at least, a sin so venial, that God will not take cognizance of it. But you know better than this. You know that all idolaters "have their portion in the lake that burneth with fire and brimstone." You have not yet learned the art of explaining away this awful denunciation; and so long as you admit its truth, so long the consequences which I have now stated are unavoidable.

Take another view of the case. Christianity, as we receive it, is, in truth, a system of great benignity; but it is as inflexible as it is kind. It is full of mercy, but equally full of truth. The conditions upon which it offers salvation to man are as unchangeable as the nature of God; and if it only provides for the deliverance and happiness of those who embrace the atonement of Christ, it leaves those who wilfully reject that atonement under the curse of God. Nay more, its testimony upon this subject is as clear as light. "He that believeth not on the Son hath not life;" "He that believeth not is condemned already," &c.; "He that believeth not shall be damned." These, and many other passages of a like kind, the Unitarian will attempt to explain so as to evade their force; but this you cannot do. You know well what is meant by believing on the Son. You know that a reliance on his atonement is distinctly included in this phrase; and whether we are right or not, you will perceive, with our views, that it is impossible for one who rejects the atonement to obtain salvation; to such one (I speak it with deep commiseration) "there remaineth no more sacrifice for sin, but a certain fearful looking for of judgment."

You will not wonder, then, at my regret that you should be in any doubt upon this momentous doctrine. I am animated by no spirit of proselytism. I hope I am no bigot; but I cannot conceal from myself, and I dare not hide from you, what I believe will be the result of your rejection of the atonement of Christ. Again I repeat it, I have no wish to deter you from the most rigid scrutiny. Why should I, indeed, when your decision on either hand is pregnant with eternal consequences? All that I wish to impress upon you is, that this decision must not be made upon light or trivial grounds. No event of your life was so important as is your conclusion in this instance. May God give you understanding in all things!

Letter II.

My dear Friend,

You complain, that your doubts are rather increased, than lessened, by time. This is naturally to be expected. In the ordinary course of things, every revolution of sentiment is gradual; but the rapidity with which we proceed towards a conclusion, seems to increase in proportion to our nearness to it. In our doubts upon any of the great doctrines of the word of God, this is easily accounted for. I suggested to you, in my last letter, that the immediate effect of the doubts which at present affect you, was the deadening of your devotional exercises. The result of restraining prayer before God is an increase of the pride and perverseness of the heart, of which, in our best moments, we have too great reason to complain. This, in its turn, goes to augment the power of our doubts; and thus, by mutual action, we are hurried into a rejection of doctrines, upon which, at one time, we believed our eternal interests to depend.

You are startled and shocked by the suggestions of my last letter. This is as it should be. Your great danger is, lest you should be imperceptibly carried away by the influence of your doubts. This, at least, is no longer possible. You see the gulf before you. Your eyes are, in some degree, open to your peril; and it will now require a measure of recklessness to make the plunge, which you cannot yet attain. But let me inquire, my dear friend, whether this increase of doubt, this augmented agitation of mind, does not appear to you to supply a considerable presumption in favour of the doctrine of the atonement. You admit that your enjoyment of secret devotion is considerably diminished; and you appear also to be aware, that your doubts increase as your delight in prayer is lessened. Does it not then appear sufficiently manifest that these doubts are evils? and evils, too, of no ordinary magnitude? Is it to be supposed, that an increasing desire for the truth would render you reluctant to apply to the fountain of all truth? Can the increasing wish to do the will of God actually unfit you for doing that will? This, you readily admit, is impossible; and it follows, therefore, that your present state of mind is not the result of such desires as these, but of the operation of some principle. which is displeasing to God, and pernicious to you.

You will recollect, that, in some of our conversations on infidelity, we have remarked, that the state of a man's belief is, to a considerable degree, dependent upon the condition of his moral feeling. If you have ever recurred to this sentiment, I do not doubt that you have seen that it accords with facts more fully than, at the first blush, one should be disposed to believe. In your present state of mind, I fear, that my reminding you of it will not be very welcome; and yet it is undoubtedly applicable to you. You feel that you have experienced some deterioration of religious character; and you find that your doubts upon the questions of the divinity and atonement of Christ are proportioned to it. It is possible, therefore, in the regular process of things, that you may arrive at a state of unbelief so confirmed, that were I now to describe it, you would shrink in horror, and exclaim, "Is thy servant a dog, that he should do this thing?" Happy indeed will it be for you, if you pause in your course, to retrace your steps;—happy, if, beholding your danger, you seek refuge under the shadow of the Almighty.

I augur well, indeed, from your inquiry:— "In the multitude of conflicting opinions upon the subject of the atonement, how am I to arrive at anything like certainty upon this momentous question?" This you ask in sincerity, I know; and, as far as I am able, I will answer you.

The doctrine of the atonement, if it be true, is to be found in the Bible, and in the Bible only. If God had not revealed it, we should never have conjectured anything resembling it. It is quite beyond the scope and range of human reason; and human reason, therefore, has obviously no share in its discovery or elaboration. Reason has its own sphere; and while restrained there, and properly employed, it will exalt and ennoble man; but if allowed to trespass on realms which revelation alone can explore, it will prove a treacherous and destructive guide. We are all fully aware of the respective bounds of several sciences, or systems of truth; and no one is so silly as to suppose, that, because a man is acquainted with one, therefore he is capable of discussing the whole. History we know from testimony; truth of some kinds we ascertain by induction; while a third sort of knowledge is secured by experiment. But what should we think of a man who supposed himself perfectly qualified to decide upon a question in politics, because he understood conic sections? Still more absurd is it for reason to intrude on the province of revelation; and for us to attempt to determine whether or not any doctrine is probable which is made known in the word of God.

If there be a revelation, it must declare to us truths, which, without it, we should not have known. The all-wise God does nothing in vain; and it is certain that, had we been able to ascertain everything requisite to salvation by the exercise of unassisted reason, we should have been left to our own discoveries. We have not been so left; and it is therefore obvious that, in the Bible, we are to expect truths, strange, startling, and mysterious. I say "mysterious; for that which reason cannot discover, it is natural to conclude, reason cannot fully comprehend. We are bewildered, indeed, in what we do discover by the exercise of our reason. A blade of grass puzzles us. Of the law of gravitation, which we feel every instant, we understand next to nothing. Not a grain of sand, nor a particle of light, nor a drop of water, are capable of fully explaining; and every atom of matter possesses properties which the united philosophy of six thousand years has not yet divested of mystery. The conclusion, therefore, is obvious: if that which is palpable to our senses, and which we have a thousand times most accurately examined, and which has been examined by the most profound science which the world ever supplied, is yet capable of evading our researches, and compelling us to confess our ignorance, how can we, without the grossest folly and arrogance, suppose ourselves able to judge conclusively, and to comprehend fully, what we should never have conjectured, had not God mercifully made it known to us?

Does it not occur to you also, that, independently of the comparative imperfection of our intellectual powers, there is another reason for the mysteriousness of revelation, to be found in the moral condition of man, in the present state? We are now in a condition of probation; we admit the existence of a scheme of probation in matters purely moral; we feel that nothing can be more wise or righteous, nothing more honourable to God, or more illustrative of human dignity, than that the destinies of eternity shall depend upon a process of moral trial in time.

But upon what principle shall we restrict this law to man as a moral being? Are we not to believe, that the present is equally a state of intellectual probation? Were the fact otherwise, there is great reason to believe, either that the communications of God to his intelligent creatures would have been more ample, or that their capacities would have been sufficiently enlarged to enable them to embrace more comprehensive views of those truths actually revealed. It nearly amounts to a moral certainty, that God might, even with our present powers, have made known much more than he has done; and that what he has made known might have been presented to us in a more detailed and systematized form. If this is indeed the fact, there are but two reasons, I think, which we can assign for withholding such information: the one is, that the revelation which we actually possess is sufficient for all purposes of moral improvement, and upon this it was the design of God that our attention should be concentrated; and the other, that it was fitting that man should learn as fully to submit his understanding as his heart to the simple declaration of Scripture. These reasons, though differing in themselves, nevertheless lead to the same conclusion, and instruct us in the same truth, and that is,—that it is absurd and presumptuous for us to expect to be able, in this life, to comprehend the great subjects of which revelation alone can inform us, and respecting which revelation itself only supplies us with partial instruction.

The future condition of the saint will, no doubt, be distinguished by amazing intellectual accessions; we shall see eye to eye; we shall know even as we are known. But as certainly as the future shall be a state of vision, so certainly is the present a condition expressly designed for the exercise of faith. But if there were no mystery in religious doctrine; if there were nothing but what reason could completely apprehend; and if man could attain upon all subjects connected with the divine government the most ample information; it is obvious that there would be no room for the exercise of faith. It is not a subject of faith that two right angles are equal to a triangle; because this is demonstrable. We do not believe that the sun rose today; we know it. There is no virtue in our admitting such facts, because we cannot reject them. But faith is a virtue, a virtue of fundamental character; as such it is always represented in the Bible; but it can only be deemed so upon the supposition, that it is possible for us to refuse to honour God by its exercise. We may disbelieve the truths contained in the Bible. It is in the highest degree fitting that we should possess this power; otherwise, our probation would be exceedingly incomplete, since it would not extend to our intellectual nature; and the removal of mystery from theology, and especially the theology of the Bible, instead of causing an increase of light, would, in fact, shed disastrous eclipse upon the glory of God's government of a race of intelligent and rational beings.

Has God given me a revelation? Then I must believe it, and that entirely and without reserve, as well what is unaccountable and mysterious, as what is clear and comprehensible. No dictate of reason can be more distinct and peremptory than that which requires my faith to every iota of the testimony of God. No sin against reason can be so glaring as unbelief. The obligation to receive all that God has declared does not result from any capability of my own understanding to investigate and comprehend, but from the simple fact, that whatever God reveals must be true. Truth is as eternal and immutable as His nature from whom it emanates; but my reason is vacillating, feeble, and obscure. Unfitted, therefore, as I am, to decide upon the great questions of religious belief and obligation, it is my highest wisdom to embrace the word of God as my unerring guide. This, then, it is my determination to do; and thus do I design to vindicate my claims to the character of rationality. It may please God to heap calamities upon my head more aggravated and painful than I can now conceive; my lot may be shame and sorrow through a long series of years; but let him not leave me to myself; let him not seal his book against me; let him not deliver me over to blindness of understanding, or hardness of heart; and whatever else may befall me, I am content to endure it, and wait the result in a better and purer state.

But you will probably inquire whether reason is of no use in matters of religion. It undoubtedly is; for how, except by its proper exercise, can we ascertain that the system professing to be divine is duly evidenced to be such? and how, except by the same employment of our reason, are we to apprehend the meaning of the divine testimony? These, you will admit, are not only questions to be appreciated by the employment of my rational faculties, but sufficient also to admit of their fullest exertion. Look at the gigantic intellects which have been employed in stating and elaborating the evidences of Christianity, and the various doctrines which are essential to its existence and perpetuation. The concentrated energies of their lives have been directed to these subjects; and, however human philosophy may have dignified its votaries, it is not too much to affirm, that the mind of man has never been so nobly occupied, or so signally distinguished, as when elucidating the glorious verities of the Christian faith. This, it is probable, will be a portion of the employment of restored and immortal spirits, when death shall have been "swallowed up in victory." And if eternity cannot supply any more lofty intellectual occupation, surely it is not too much to affirm, that it is sufficient for man in his present imperfect condition. It need not, then, be matter of complaint, that God has sealed up our intellects in darkness and silence, by the revelation of his word; on the contrary, while he has thus rendered unnecessary the speculations of vain and inflated minds, he has opened to the humble, however intellectually capacious and energetic, a field of contemplation too ample to be fully traced till the shadows of mortality flee away, and we stand upon the mount of eternal and unimpeded vision.

Nor is this all, since, to a certain extent, our reason may be profitably employed in searching into the reasons of the divine conduct and counsel. All research of this kind must, it is true, be conducted with immediate and constant reference to the testimony of revelation; and even then we shall certainly meet with much that is mysterious. Yet we need not scruple to affirm, that we may ascertain the grounds of the divine government quite as fully as is required for all practical purposes. Into questions of curious speculation we are not invited to enter; but so far as it is possible for intellectual man, in his present state, to appreciate the divine counsels, in order to bring the perfect approbation of the understanding, as well as the entire devotion of the heart, to the service of God, so far may we trace the reason of those arrangements of which the Bible testifies; and this, I think you will admit, is all that we can rationally require.

It is the remark of a celebrated modern philosopher, that the mind of man delights in analogies; and for this peculiar appetite, God, in his mercy, has made very extensive provision. Some of these are to be found even in the natural world; and others in those facts of the moral government of God which are palpable to our senses, and open to daily observation. Some of them are purely illustrative; others seem to be, also, confirmatory, not as rendering the testimony of God more certain, but as strengthening our imperfect belief. Thus far has our gracious Creator condescended to our infirmities. The Bible supplies us with many analogical suggestions, both for the clearer elucidation, and for the more abundant confirmation, of its truths; while the course of things around us supplies us with others: and so far as the most trivial incident of human life tends to shed fresh light upon the truth of revelation, or to confirm our faith in it, so far we may fairly gather, that the institution of such analogies is a very proper and advantageous employment of our intellectual faculties.

On these several modes of employing reason in matters pertaining to revelation I shall have occasion to remark hereafter. My present communication has been protracted beyond my original design, and here therefore I take my leave.

Letter III.

My dear Friend,

In my last letter I alluded to the employ of reason in matters of revelation. This, you will recollect, respected, 1. Christian evidences. 2. Interpretation. 3. The grounds of the divine conduct. And, 4. Analogy. In discussing any doctrine supposed to be stated in Scripture, it is, of course, desirable, and even necessary, that there should be, on all hands, a clear understanding of the weight attributed to the evidences of the inspiration of the Bible, and that there should be admitted a common scheme of interpretation. It is not in all cases required, that there should be a specific reference to these topics; because among certain classes of Christians they are distinctly understood and unhesitatingly received in the same sense. In the case before us, however, as you will perceive from the sequel, it is needful that we should be more minute, and that we should draw some conclusions from these subjects, which may serve to confirm propositions already stated, and to prepare your mind for other views which I shall hereafter have occasion to bring before you.

I think it not improbable that you may have been struck with the stupendous character of Scripture miracles, and the great variety and minuteness of Scripture prophecy. Indeed, it is scarcely possible that you should have directed your attention to these subjects at all without having received this impression. But the peculiarity to which I wish particularly to call your observation is, the succession of these wonders for so many ages, and the considerable number of individuals gifted with the extraordinary power which they imply. You will remark, that it is incontestably evident, that from the time of Moses, (to go no higher,) down to the period when Christianity had obtained a considerable footing in the world, there were, with some intermission, individuals whom God empowered to attract the attention of mankind, by the working of miracles, and the prediction of future events. It may indeed consist with the wisdom of man to employ mighty agencies for the production of inconsiderable results; but it is a remark not more trite than true, that it is the divine plan to reverse that method, and to educe the grandest events from causes and by means exceedingly simple, and apparently insignificant.

What then is the system of truth for the ascertaining of which the grand succession of miracles and prophecy was appointed? Does it merely consist of doctrines which equally belong to what is called "natural religion," and which are more or less discoverable by the proper exercise of our natural faculties? This is not to be supposed, since it would involve the conclusion, that the whole of the miraculous and prophetic gifts which go to accredit the truth of Scripture were not only insignificant, but absolutely useless. Suppose a man were to write a number of volumes to prove some fact in science with which mankind at large were either fully acquainted, or readily might become so,—say on the theory of eclipses; suppose that he were to spend his life in wandering from one country to another, to demonstrate what every tyro in astronomy understood as fully as himself; suppose he were at vast expense to construct a number of magnificent orreries, and to employ the whole of a princely fortune in these and similar employments; suppose he were to make it obligatory upon his children to spend their time and strength for a similar purpose, and make arrangements which should extend to all posterity for instructing mankind in a few facts in philosophy, which no one at all doubts: what would be your conclusion?

Remark, then, the impiety of that system which attributes to the all-wise God the institution of stupendous means, and those maintained for ages, in order to teach men what they might all have known without any such agencies. Say that the miracles of Scripture, and its prophecies, are only designed to authenticate a system of ethics, or to render the doctrine of man's immortality more certain than it otherwise would have appeared, and what contempt and dishonour do you thus cast upon the divine counsels, and to what a low and dishonoured place do you reduce Him whose glory is infinite and eternal! To my own mind there is something exceedingly shocking in the notion of the gratuitous exhibition of the divine power, which some self-called "rational Christians" nevertheless appear greatly to delight in. If any doctrine required to be certified by a miracle, or without a miracle would have failed to impress the minds of men, it is obvious that mere reason is insufficient in matters of religion; while if reason can enable us to discover or to determine upon such subjects, the whole scheme of Scripture miracles and prophecy is absolutely useless.

To this latter conclusion I am convinced you cannot bring yourself to assent. The other, therefore, is the only alternative. Nay, more, it is clear that not only reason is insufficient in matters of religion, but that the discoveries of revelation must be in the highest degree extraordinary and supernatural. It appears as if God had condescended to human infirmity, and had provided against that unbelief which would naturally present itself to the testimony of his word. Had we in our researches in revealed truth met with the most mysterious doctrines in every page, — doctrines of themselves utterly incredible, and only here and there with a solitary wonder to repress our doubt and infidelity, it would have required a higher order of virtue than we are in the habit of practising, to submit our understandings fully to the divine testimony. But God, in mercy, has not thus tried us. Though one well- authenticated exhibition of his power in attestation of any doctrine ought to be sufficient, and upon a perfectly pure mind would be sufficient, yet in compassion to our tendencies to unbelief, he has crowded wonder upon wonder. He has taxed every element for our satisfaction, till the mysteries of Scripture appear less startling than its miracles, and the history of the Bible has become the marvellous counterpoise of its theology. Since, therefore, God has taken such pains (if I may so express myself) to render his word credible, it must in all reason be concluded that, independent of these extraordinary accompaniments, it would have been beyond our power of belief. If, therefore, any scheme for the interpretation of Scripture robs it of its extraordinary character, and claims only a degree of submission which we should readily have offered in the absence of miraculous testimony, we may certainly conclude that such a scheme is fundamentally erroneous.

    This reasoning will readily suggest to you the feelings with which we ought to go to the examination of what is called the internal evidence of Christianity; that sort of testimony of its divine origin which is derived from the doctrines, morals, and harmony of the Bible. It is not enough that the truths of Scripture are sublime, that its precepts are pure, and that its parts are harmonious. It must instruct us in what we should never have remotely conjectured without its aid; it must transcend all that is wonderful of which we have ever heard or dreamed; it must be systematized by the influence of truths unequivocally supernatural; and, in short, it must be essentially correspondent in its marvellous character with the grand and startling series of miracles by which it is accredited.

Now this is precisely the sort of Christianity which you have hitherto believed, and the doubts by which you are this moment agitated respect a doctrine which, if withdrawn from the Bible, will take away everything extraordinary from the system which the Bible teaches, will absolutely destroy the internal evidences of its divinity, and will reduce all miracles and prophecy to mere idle and contemptible irregularities of nature. But if you cannot allow yourself to come to this conclusion, how can you justify anything approaching to scepticism upon that great truth, which alone can prevent you from arriving at it?

You will now, I think, be able to appreciate the use of reason in examining the evidences of revelation. Suffer me, therefore, to call your attention to the subject of Scripture interpretation, as another of the methods in which our reason may be profitably employed. The Bible is manifestly intended for universal benefit, and must, therefore, be translated into all languages. The fairest, and indeed, the only justifiable mode of translation, is the literal rendering of every phrase of the original, so far as it will not interfere with the idiom of the people for whose use the translation may be designed. Fidelity is the first quality of a good translation; simplicity and perspicuity, the only important requisites besides. With these views, it is certainly possible that the Bible may be rendered into all dialects under heaven, with the assurance that in the main it will produce the same impression as to its meaning. There is, in fact, no conceivable reason for any other mode of rendering the Bible into modern languages, any more than in the case of ancient writers generally; and if this be the rule for Herodotus or Livy, there is no ground for departing from it in the case of Moses and Paul.

Now, translation is one species of interpretation; and the plan adopted in reference to it must be adhered to in every other sort of interpretation. If it be needful to supply explanations of any part of the Bible, it can only be effected by assuming that the terms employed by its writers are accordant with the ordinary usages of language. This is the more requisite, because, if there be any class of persons for whose especial use the Scripture is designed, it is the poor and illiterate. Of this fact the whole tenor of the New Testament assures us. With the popular acceptation of the language of the sacred writers, these individuals are tolerably familiar; but if any other mode of interpretation be employed, they are unavoidably cut off from all interest in that book which is peculiarly intended for their advantage. To abandon the rule here proposed, therefore, is not only unreasonable, but cruel. The resources of the rich and the cultivated are numerous; but if you rob the poor man of his birth-right, and deprive him of spiritual consolation—if you destroy that which sanctifies the cottage—if you darken the chamber of affliction, and dash the cup of peace from the lips of the dying—your act is a thousand times more wicked than any sin against the liberties and secular rights of men in other circumstances. No terms of reprobation, therefore, are too strong to characterize that sort of interpretation which sets aside the ordinary usages of language in the case of the writers of the Bible.

Besides, if it be admitted that the Bible is not to be interpreted in this way, it is obvious that the subject is incapable of any sort of rule. Henceforth, all is confusion and doubt; and where is the mind that is to arbitrate between ten thousand contending interpreters? Every man, it is clear, has a right to explain the Bible, and each must explain it in his own way, only avoiding the literal and plain meaning of its declarations. No fancy would be too gross, no fanaticism too ferocious or ridiculous, and no licentiousness too glaring, to find some support in the Bible, when thus tortured according to the depraved imaginations of men. You know well what impiety and folly have already resulted from an abandonment of the plain declarations of Scripture. And if the church has been so afflicted with heresy and fanaticism, while the same common-sense law of interpretation generally obtained, it requires no great sagacity to conjecture the monstrous results of compelling men universally to abjure the ordinary meaning of words, and to discover some remote and arbitrary explanation of them. In this case, the Bible, instead of being a blessing to society, would, in reality, be its greatest curse, since it might readily be made to afford a sanction to the most outrageous vices, and the name and word of God employed to countenance a contempt of all decency, morality, and good order; while every attempt to repress these pernicious errors would be denounced as persecution, oppression, and tyranny. If it be too much to suppose that this would be universally the case, it is easy to perceive that the ordinary refuge of common sense would be in an utter rejection of the Bible. This could hardly fail to result from the prevalence of wild and unauthorized interpretation of Scripture; and the whole of society would thus be divided into fanatics, antinomians, and infidels.

 If the literal explanation of the Bible be not the true one, it will follow either that its writers were incapable of expressing themselves intelligibly, or that they were indifferent to the effects of their writings upon society. And to which of these conclusions must we resort? The one is, that they were all but idiots; the other, that they were anything but honest men. I confess, I am at a loss which of these opinions to prefer. They are both so absurd, and, I may add, so wicked, that it is difficult to decide upon their respective probabilities. Either of them renders the Bible incredible; and to either, undisguised infidelity is, in my judgment, far preferable. That God would employ men to communicate his truth to all ages of the church, who were literally fools, or worse; that he would substantiate their claims by the most surprising miracles; and that he would condemn all who rejected their testimony to eternal misery;—are propositions so monstrous, that no sane man will for a moment credit them. There is, therefore, no alternative between an entire rejection of Scripture, and an admission that its writers were both capable of expressing themselves intelligibly, and deeply concerned that their statements should be correctly understood. The only conclusion, therefore, to which a believer in the authority of the Bible can arrive is, that it is to be interpreted in its plainest and most obvious sense. Take an example:—

It is not to be denied, that, at the present moment, the Christian church, with a very few exceptions, consists of worshippers of Christ. Millions, once a week at least, join in addressing "God the Son, Redeemer of the world," and exclaiming, "Thou art the King of Glory, O Christ! thou art the everlasting Son of the Father." This we know has been the case for many ages. But if Christ be not really God, all such persons are idolaters. Yet they find a series of scriptures which, when explained in their most obvious sense, appear to sanction this worship. If, therefore, the doctrine of Christ's divinity be heresy, it is very plain that it originated in the equivocal statements of the writers of the Bible: and this brings us back to our former position; these persons must have been incapable of expressing themselves definitely, or they must have been careless whether the church became almost wholly alienated from God, or remained firmly attached to his worship; whether it dedicated its best adoration to the one true God, or to a human being; whether, in short, they became the means of establishing a system of idolatry more plausible, and more likely to prevail, than any of which the world had ever before conceived.

You will be prepared, I think, to go with me even further than this, and to admit, that if the Bible is not to be interpreted according to the natural signification of its phraseology, it must have been designed to deceive the bulk of mankind. Human nature in all ages is the same; and the habits of the mind in interpretation are precisely what they were when St. John wrote his Gospel. Of course, therefore, it must have been clear to the writers of the Bible, that what they asserted would be understood in the most literal sense of which their statements were capable. Under this impression they must have written, and the result is plain enough in the present opinions of the mass of Christians. Since, therefore, we cannot deny the writers of Scripture an ordinary measure of common sense, it follows that they must have intended to produce the present state of things; and if our doctrines be untrue, that they must have intended to delude mankind and dishonour God. And yet there are those who reject the ordinary interpretation of their statements, who, nevertheless, believe that they were divinely commissioned; in other words, that God sanctioned the efforts of wicked men to deceive the world; that he enabled them to work many miracles for the product of the most compact and enduring system of idolatry which ever existed. But I cannot proceed. The impiety and absurdity of this unavoidable conclusion is so palpable, so rank, so shocking, that I cannot bring myself to prosecute it any further. Infidelity is wicked enough, but hardly so outrageous as this. It is, at least, more consistent; and, of consequence, preferable.

To sum up these arguments:

1. The Bible was intended for all mankind, and particularly for the poor and illiterate. But it can be of no use except upon the admission, that all men are capable of understanding its contents; and this they cannot be but according to the natural signification of its statements.

2. The Bible was designed to be a universal moral blessing. This design can only be accomplished by a common rule of interpretation. But if it be not understood according to the ordinary use of language, there can be no such rule; and, in that case, it becomes the most pernicious book in the world.

3. God has given his sanction to the writers of the Bible. They must, therefore, have been both intellectually and morally qualified for their task. They could not have intended to deceive men; nor could they have been unaware of the meaning which would be attributed to their writings. The doctrines, therefore, which they have been generally supposed to state, must be such as they designed us to receive. But these doctrines are gathered from the literal interpretation of their statements: therefore, they must have intended us to understand their writings according to the natural signification of their phraseology.

Now to apply this reasoning to the doctrine of the atonement of Christ, the question you will perceive is, simply, whether this doctrine, as generally received, may be gathered from the natural signification of the Scriptures. Can we, while we keep in view the ordinary modes of language, find in the Bible any declarations which amount to an assurance that the death of Christ was a vicarious sacrifice? Did he suffer in our stead? Did he die that we might be saved from the punishment due to our sins? Was his death rendered necessary by the inflexibility of divine justice; and did he by this act satisfy the requisitions of justice, so that our sins might thus be forgiven? I have designedly put these interrogatories in those forms of words which are popularly employed upon this subject; not because they are not capable of objection from captious minds, but because they are, on the whole, more appropriate and intelligible than any perfectly novel mode of phraseology. In reply, then, out of multitudes of passages, take the following: — "Surely he hath borne our griefs, and carried our sorrows: yet we did esteem him stricken, smitten of God, and afflicted. But he was wounded for our transgressions, he was bruised for our iniquities: the chastisement of our peace was upon him, and with his stripes we are healed." (Isai. liii. 4-6.) "For when we were yet without strength, in due time Christ died for the ungodly. But God commendeth his love toward us, in that, while we were yet sinners, Christ died for us. And not only so, but we also joy in God through our Lord Jesus Christ, by whom we have now received the atonement." (Rom. v. 6, 8, 11.) "In whom we have redemption through his blood, the forgiveness of sins, according to the riches of his grace." (Eph. i. 7.) "And that he might reconcile both unto God in one body by the cross, having slain the enmity thereby." (ii. 16.) "Walk in love, as Christ also hath loved us, and hath given himself for us an offering and a sacrifice to God for a sweet-smelling savour." (v. 2.) "One mediator between God and men, the man Christ Jesus; who gave himself a ransom for all, to be testified in due time." (1 Tim. i. 5, 6.) "For Christ also hath once suffered for sins, the just for the unjust, that he might bring us to God, being put to death in the flesh, but quickened by the Spirit. Who is gone into heaven, and is on the right hand of God; angels and authorities and powers being made subject unto him." (1 Pet. iii. 18, 22.)

And here I might pause. It is enough that the Bible abounds with such declarations as these. I need not tell you what is their obvious signification; and, if you have any suspicion as to the correctness of the translation, you may refer to the originals, and satisfy yourself. This I believe you will not think necessary; but should you take the pains to do so, you will find that, however these passages *may* be rendered, their plain signification is conveyed in our version, and, as already shown, this is the only mode of interpretation which is at all allowable. I recommend these and the like statements of the sacred Scriptures to your most devotional meditation; and I trust that you will be enabled to acquire that, temper of mind in which you shall take refuge from all doubts, in the simple recognition of the truth of God's most holy word.

Yet I think it may not be improper to direct your attention to other arguments and considerations upon this momentous question. Were the assaults of its opponents confined to the mode of interpreting certain passages of Scripture, this course might not be needful; but as they offer suggestions upon other grounds, it will be desirable for you to perceive that we have also a sufficient variety of defensive weapons to enable us to meet their attack with perfect calmness and certain triumph.

Letter IV.

MY DEAR FRIEND,

I AM GLAD TO FIND that the arguments which I have already suggested to you have afforded you any degree of satisfaction. I now most readily resume the subject, and, according to the statement at the conclusion of my last letter, propose to adduce some additional views for the illustration and vindication of the scriptural doctrine of the atonement. There are, I think, three sorts of arguments which go to support this doctrine. The first is that derived from the fact, that without it salvation is unattainable; the second is suggested by analogy; and the third is founded upon the harmony of the doctrine in itself, and with the general tenor of Scripture. To each of these I propose to devote a separate consideration.

The first grand argument in favour of the orthodox view of the atonement is derived from its necessity to the salvation of man. That our salvation is essentially connected with something which Christ has taught or done, will not be doubted by any who believe the Bible. "Neither is there salvation in any other: for there is none other name under heaven given among men, whereby we must be saved." (Acts iv. 12.) "For other foundation can no man lay than that is laid, which is Jesus Christ." (1 Cor. iii. 11.) Now, if these passages be explained as referring merely to the doctrines which Christ taught, it is not true, in any sense, that there is not salvation in any other, since many others have taught the same doctrines, and have taught them far more amply than Christ did. But nothing can be clearer, than that the sacred writers represent salvation to result from the work of Christ exclusively, and with a peculiarity of emphasis and distinction. This is to be discovered in the text just quoted. It must be recollected, that the word "name" was employed by the Hebrews to signify not merely what is "distinct," but what is "eminent." The word שם, which is so rendered in the Old Testament, Schultens derives from the Arabic verb שמה or שמא — "to be high, elevated," or "eminent;" hence eminent men are called שמות אבשי, "men of names." (1 Chron. v. 24; xii. 30.)

Hence, in the victory over Gog, prophesied of by Ezekiel, it is said, that it shall be to the triumphant host "a name," or, as the authorized version renders it, "a renown;" (Ezek. xxxix. 13;) and in a prophecy of Christ, by the same Prophet, it is said, "I will raise for them a plant of renown," that is, for name. (xxxiv. 29.) Thus "the name of the Lord" is a phrase designed to describe his eminence and majesty.— "The name of the Lord is a strong tower." (Prov. xviii. 10.) "They that know thy name will put their trust in thee." (Psal. ix. 10.) "But let all those that put their trust in thee rejoice: let them ever shout for joy, because thou defendest them: let them also that love thy name be joyful in thee." (v. 11.) "O LORD our Lord, how excellent is thy name in all the earth!" (viii. 1.) "Through thy name," that is, strength," will we tread them under that rise up against us." (xliv. 5.) "According to thy name," that is, majesty, "so is thy praise unto the ends of the earth." (xlviii. 10.) "That thy name," that is, power, "is near, thy wondrous works declare." (lxxv. 1.) In these, and many other places of the Jewish Scriptures, the sacred writers employ the word "name" to describe those attributes which are peculiar to Jehovah; and, as in the passage now under consideration, we find the word employed by a Jewish preacher, in an address to a Jewish congregation, the conclusion is, that some peculiarity in the work of Christ, something eminent and distinctive, is intended. But this could not be his doctrine, since, as we have already remarked, in that others shared; and of its truths, in their most comprehensive form, others were more fully the preachers than himself. The salvation which Christ supplies results from what he alone did; from a work in which he had no assistant or coadjutor; and what this work is, cannot be conjectured, except it be allowed to be his great vicarious sacrifice and atonement.

But if this mode of reasoning does not satisfy you, it will not be difficult to suggest another, to which I think you will hardly object. Allow, for the sake of argument, that the Apostle Peter only meant to say that there was no other system of doctrine and morals, but that taught by Christ, which could supply men with salvation, it will follow, that he that does not cordially believe that doctrine, nor fully practise that morality, cannot be saved. And where is the man that can cherish the slightest hope of salvation upon these terms? Let our Lord's sermon upon the mount be the test of our morality, and who can be saved? Where is the man whose heart has been universally free from anger, covetousness, resentment, and distrust of God's providence? whose lips have never been employed, except to bless his enemies, to adore his God, to express universal charity? Where is the eye that has never shot an impure glance, or the slightest expression of malevolence, under the greatest provocation? Where is the hand which has never been employed in wrath or covetousness? Alas! every mouth is stopped, and all the world is guilty before God; and there certainly is no salvation for man upon such terms as these.

It seems, indeed, almost impossible that any man should be able to close his ears, I will not say against the testimony of Scripture, but against the testimony of universal experience, upon the subject of the entire corruption of human nature. For if it be allowed that all have sinned, which no one who believes the Bible will question, there is no other mode in which this momentous fact can be accounted for. To attribute it to example, is only to remove the difficulty one generation, and the depravity of the exemplars is just as unaccountable as that of their posterity; and thus we may go back to the first man, and we shall then be more at a loss than ever. Example, at least, could have nothing to do with him. To suppose that his immediate posterity were corrupted by his example, if he were a pure being, is nonsense; and to admit him not to have been pure, is, in fact, to allow that very principle of evil of which the Scripture testifies. And if the first of men was the subject of a real depravation of nature, it must be allowed that his posterity cannot be rationally supposed free from it. Beyond this, they have the influence of example as a secondary, though incalculably powerful, cause of impurity; and, superadded to both in the bulk of mankind, a sinful system of education confirms the one, and increases the power of the other.

To a mind philanthropically disposed it is a question of painful interest: "How can man be just with God, and how can he be clean that is born of a woman?" We are at no loss for a reply; but what are the resources of the rejecters of the doctrine of the atonement? It will not be affirmed by any who admit a system of divine government, that God will forgive sin merely as a matter of prerogative. If he pass by all sin, he ceases to be a governor in any conceivable sense of the term; and if he forgive some arbitrarily, and leave the rest to perish, he ceases to be an equitable governor. But as neither of these conclusions can be allowed, some other method must be suggested for human justification.

By all who reject the notion of the forgiveness of sin by the arbitrary constitution of the divine will, the doctrine of substitution is either tacitly or avowedly admitted; that is, they acknowledge that the Governor of the universe accepts something instead of the actual punishment of the sinner. Those who reject the atonement usually put repentance in its room. Hence Socinus expressly affirms, that the pardon of an impenitent sinner is inconsistent with equity; and Dr. Priestley, when arguing upon the freeness of the pardon which the Gospel proclaims, confines it to the "truly penitent." Now, if by "repentance," be merely meant sorrow for sin, this notion, after all, resolves the pardon of the offender into an act of the divine prerogative, since it is certain that there is no man who, at one time or other of his life, does not regret the commission of sin. All men, therefore, according to this opinion, will be freed from punishment; which is absurd.

In order, therefore, to relieve themselves from this difficulty, some of our rational theologues add "amendment of life" to "repentance;" and teach, that God will forgive all past offences upon the condition that we offend no more. It is true that we have no idea of a government, in this world, conducted on such principles; but that, it would appear, is of no importance to the argument. It is true that we cannot conceive how any past acts can be at all affected by our future conduct. The debauchee may become chaste, but this does not restore the health which he has lost by his licentious life; the prodigal may become frugal, but this does not give him back his squandered patrimony; the dishonest man may forsake his fraudulent courses, but he cannot retrieve his forfeited reputation; but the sinner, we are told, if he only cease to sin, will escape all the consequences of his past transgression. And is this credible? Is it possible, upon the bare mention of such an opinion, that any one should be blind to its utter and melancholy absurdity? He does his duty now, therefore he shall be regarded as having always done his duty; he ceaseth to sin, therefore he shall be treated as though he had never sinned. This, also, you will perceive, resolves the pardon of sin into an act of the divine prerogative. The only difference is, that, in this latter instance, it is not the sins of the whole life, but only of a part of life, that are to be forgiven. If a man sins on, and dies at thirty without amendment, he is to be punished; but if he goes on sinning till sixty, and then reforms, he is to be forgiven, and to be placed upon the level of a being who has never sinned. No matter how short a time he lives; a day of reformation shall cancel the multiplied offences of sixty years; nay, the sincere resolution to amend, if there be no opportunity for carrying it into effect, must be esteemed sufficient to commend him to the divine mercy, and to introduce him into an immortality of happiness. A most comfortable doctrine, truly!

Amendment of life, you will perceive, by this theory, is represented as sufficiently meritorious to induce the Governor of all to regard him in whom he finds it, as exonerated from all obligation for the time that is past; because, if this be not the case, the obligation must still remain, and the breach of this obligation must be precisely as guilty as if no amendment had taken place. But if it is possible for a man hereafter to be relieved from an obligation which oppresses him now, it is difficult for him to suppose that it is of much importance, and impossible to believe that the obligations to virtue are otherwise than exceedingly variable. Or, to take another view of the subject, a man cannot be supposed to be under any obligation to perfect purity of life, because the fulfilment of to-day's obligations can discharge a man from the guilt of having neglected those of yesterday. And if a virtuous course of life may have a retrospective influence, there is no reason why it may not operate prospectively; and hence one may lay in a stock of good works that will satisfactorily relieve one from any need to be virtuous hereafter. And if the amendment of a year or a day can cancel the obligation and the guilt of half a century, or more, it is very comfortable to reflect how short a time it is necessary to remain virtuous, to enable one to sin with impunity for the rest of one's life.

Besides, you will at once see that there is no proportion in this doctrine. Equity not only has to do with punishment and reward, but with the proportions of each. If a day's or a year's virtue will remove the guilt of a long life, all farther observation of the divine law is needless; and if deeply aggravated guilt only requires entire amendment, less venial guilt may be relieved by a less rigorous morality. An eminent transgressor must be severely virtuous; a medium sinner will not require any reformation at all. However much the one may reform, he will scarcely arrive at an equilibrium with the other, who does not amend in any degree; and, at the close of life, the actual and unchanged sinner will have, in the aggregate, less guilt than the man who, for some little while, has been a model of piety. This, at least, ought to be the case, according to ordinary notions of justice; but this the theory in question will not allow. Amendment is an essential to salvation: and hence, though both are said to be dealt with on the ground of merit, the least meritorious is saved, and the other perishes.

But perhaps it will be replied, that God remits the sin of a reformed offender on the ground of pure mercy and benevolence. Then, upon the same ground, he may remit all sin, since unmingled mercy does not respect any quality in the recipient. To this it will be urged, that there is no fitness in such a procedure. True;

but that brings us back to the former position. An amended sinner, therefore, must be pardoned on the score of equity, and then all the foregoing absurdities still attach themselves to the theory.

Waving for one moment, however, all these preposterous conclusions, let us inquire, what is the sort of amendment for which the advocates of this opinion contend? Is it merely the reformation of the life, while the sins of the mind are still allowed to predominate? This will hardly be affirmed; but if not, is man able of himself to cleanse his own heart? Can the spirit which has long lived in an atmosphere of pride, and of vainglory, compel itself down into the deep of humiliation and self-distrust? Can the covetous mind alienate itself from its longings, and become, by its own effort, contented and tranquil? Can the impure heart cast off all its filthy imaginations, and render itself chaste and spiritual? Can the irascible and vindictive teach themselves to bless the hand that smites them, and to implore the smile of heaven upon the heart that curses them? Can he who "is enmity against God," by his own efforts rise into the spirit of divine love? If this be the reformation necessary to pardon, it is plainly a condition impossible to be fulfilled, except by an assistance which this doctrine repudiates. If repentance and reformation, in this acceptation, be the only method of obtaining salvation, man cannot be saved. The millions of Adam's posterity must cover their faces in despair, and go down to the darkness of hell, without possibility of escape.

I profess, if there be fallacy in this argument, I am not aware of its existence. Upon a point of such moment, no consideration should induce me to attempt to deceive you. But if the reasoning be conclusive, you will discern, without difficulty, that there is no hope for sinful man, unless it can be found in the atonement of Christ.

It cannot be too deeply impressed upon your mind, that the reasoning which goes to substantiate our view of this great doctrine is essentially different from that which is adduced in support of other theories on the same subject. The advocates of these latter are rational Christians, and their opinions are said to be indebted for their validity to reason alone. We make no such pretensions. In the sense in which this term is employed by our opponents, we have no ambition to the designation of "rational." Our claim to this title involves a different signification of it, and is based upon our willingness to render implicit faith to the testimony of God. Of course they are amenable to reason; and with whatever absurdities their opinions are encumbered, they are themselves distinctly chargeable. If our doctrines involve difficulties, we are contented to resolve them into the will of God; and though we cannot admit that there is in them anything contrary to the soundest reason, we make no pretensions to be able to divest them of what is mysterious, and of what, in our present condition, is impossible to be comprehended. On the contrary, we glory in their supernatural character, and esteem the fact of their being beyond perfect exposition, as necessary to the proof of their divinity.

We believe the doctrine of the atonement, therefore, not because we are able to comprehend it, but because, as I have already shown, we find it stated in the holy Scriptures. We do not argue on any abstract fitness in the doctrine, because that is a subject which we do not understand. We do not say that the arrangement involved in it is good, and therefore God has made it; but we resolve its propriety into divine appointment, and argue God has ordained it, and therefore it is good. Whatever arguments in favour of the doctrine may be presented to you in the course of these letters, I beseech you not to forget, that it is not upon these we ground our vindication of it. These may prove illustrative, and assist your views on the subject, or they may prove confirmatory, not of the doctrine itself, but of your faith in it. But in such a question as this, everything but the divine appointment is to be regarded as merely secondary, and, in a remote degree, subsidiary. Our wisdom, therefore, is, whenever we meet with difficulties in its discussion, or are oppressed with doubts as to its truth, to fall back upon the first principle of the argument, and to silence all doubt by the $αυτοσ εφη$, "the simple testimony of the all-wise God." I insist the more upon this, because I am led to believe that your own perplexities have arisen from a neglect of this obvious principle; and because, proceeding, as I do, to the discussion of the subject with much diffidence, I may be relieved from all distressing apprehension of the consequences of failure on my part, by the assurance that you will be able to escape all harm in the recognition of the paramount and unimpeachable authority of the divine word.

Do not imagine, however, that I make these remarks either because I suspect the doctrine in question of irrationality, or because I distrust the edge or temper of our weapons. I am most firmly convinced that the one may be commended to the highest exercise of man's understanding, and that the others are not to be evaded, except by a most unhappy obliquity of mind; and if I distrust the force of my own arm, you, at least, will not deem it any presumption against the cause of which I am an humble advocate.

I have ventured upon these general remarks, in order to introduce to you, with the more propriety, a few observations upon the connexion between the scriptural doctrine of the atonement and the pardon of the sin of man. Once more, then, I beseech you to keep in mind that I advocate the atonement as a proper method for obtaining this result, because God has so ordained it. With this recollection, you will be in no danger of misunderstanding me, or of laying undue emphasis upon the success or the failure of my reasoning.

The blessings of the Gospel are all dispensed to man by the mercy of God. The Scriptures represent the work of salvation, from first to last, as effected by grace. We have no more direct claim, upon the grounds of justice, to any good in consequence of the atonement, than we should have had in the absence of that atonement. We are commanded to repent and amend our lives, and we have imparted the power necessary to obedience; but neither repentance nor reformation produces pardon. We are commanded to trust in Christ; but neither is there any merit in the act of trust. Faith procures salvation by the appointment of God, and therefore it is right that it should produce such results; but there is no more debt to a believer on the part of God, than to an infidel. God, it is true, binds himself by his promise to connect salvation with the exercise of faith; but his promise is a promise of grace, and its fulfilment, therefore, must be an act of grace. The obligation under which our merciful Creator has laid himself, only binds him to show us favour, and not to discharge a debt; otherwise the obligation itself would have been unavoidable, — which is not to be supposed.

Now, the great object of the atonement of Christ was to demonstrate the righteousness of God, and thus to enable him, without any dishonour to his attributes and government, to show mercy to the sinner. I have before remarked, that the pardon of sin, as an act of prerogative, would practically annul the divine government. In order, therefore, that God might prove himself just as well as good, Christ was appointed to undergo, in his own person, the punishment due to our sin; not the aggregate of everlasting suffering due to the sins of all mankind, but such a measure of suffering as might illustriously evidence the purity of the divine nature, and the inflexibility of the divine law; and, as joined with the infinite dignity of the sufferer, might thus enable the Deity to bless and restore those who believe, not only without dishonour to his own character, but with an immense accession to the manifestations of his glory before the eyes of an intelligent universe.

In immediate connexion with the obedience of Christ, is a covenant by which God binds himself to reward the infinite merit of his Son. Than this, nothing could be more just; and, indeed, we can hardly conceive how such a work as that of Christ would be justly allowed to pass without an accession of infinite honour. The reward which Christ claims, is the salvation of all that believe; and as this may now be effected without disgrace to the divine law, the demand of the Saviour is ratified, and God engages thus to honour his Son to all ages. Although, therefore, as we before remarked, all the blessings shed upon us are of grace, yet the communication of such blessings to Christ, as the federal head of the faithful, is of justice; and God would, consequently, be as much dishonoured now by refusing to save those who believe, as, independently of the atonement, he would have been by the salvation of all sinners.

You will here perceive, without any difficulty, that the peculiar merit of Christ's suffering does not consist in its being merely an act of obedience to the Father, but in the demonstration which it supplies of the divine purity, by which means the highest glory is reflected upon the Deity. Upon this specific ground, it is fitting that the most exalted gifts which Christ could receive in his mixed or mediatorial character should be conferred upon him. But he seeks no greater blessedness than to be the first-born of many brethren, and to bring many sons (of God) unto glory. Thus is the design for which he suffered constituted the reward of his suffering. Thus does the Father, by the exercise of his mercy to all who believe, confer the highest honour upon the Son. The seat of the mediatorial kingdom is the paradise of God; the throne of the mediatorial kingdom is the throne of God. Here will the Father be honoured in the Son; and here will the Son be glorified by the Father; and here, when the purposes of the mediatorial work are consummated, a great multitude, which no man can number, will unite to ascribe "blessing, and honour, and glory, and power, unto Him that sitteth upon the throne, and unto the Lamb for ever and ever."

My dear friend, it is not presumptuous to hope that you and I may be admitted into this blessed society.

Letter V.

My dear Friend,

The second species of argument by which the doctrine of the atonement may be supported, is that derived from analogy. By "analogy" I mean the resemblance of relative qualities or circumstances; and, as I have before remarked, it has pleased God, in condescension to our aptness to this method of instruction, to supply us amply with analogical illustrations of his nature and government, and of the great doctrines of the Christian system. Thus, when he calls himself a Father, he employs a term of analogy, instructing us in the relation which he bears to his people by the well-known relation implied in this phrase. Thus, the relation of branches to a stock in a tree is brought before us to teach us the relation of Christ to his people. The relation of combatants is employed to illustrate the difficulties of the Christian life. In each of these analogies, you will perceive that there is no resemblance between the objects of which these relations are predicated. God does not resemble a man who has children, and who is therefore called a father;

Christ has no similarity to a tree; nor are the souls of Christians like the bodies of soldiers. The similarity you will remark is in the relation, and, even in that, only partial. There are many circumstances of the relation of a father to his children, which by no means resemble the circumstance of the relation of God to his people. The sacred writers employed the phrase in reference only to those few qualities which are common to both, and so of all others. I make these remarks here, that you may perceive that it does not at all detract from the value of analogical reasoning, that the analogous objects are totally dissimilar, and that even in their relative character they possess only a very few features of resemblance.

There are only two analogies which I propose to institute in the present instance. The one is that of typical arrangement; and the other, that of providential government. The object of each is widely different from the other. Under the first, I propose to show that there were in all ages before the coming of Christ certain religious institutions, which bore the same relation to man as a sinner, and to God as a moral governor, as the suffering of our Lord Jesus Christ is by the writers of the New Testament alleged to have done. My design, in the second of these analogies, will be to prove, from the admitted facts of the divine government, not only that it was *à priori* probable that God would employ a vicarious sacrifice for the benefit of man, but that such a proceeding can in no way detract from the perfection and righteousness of his administration.

I. In speaking on the subject of typical arrangement, your mind will at once be directed to the prevalence of animal sacrifices from the earliest periods of the history of man. That these were in one way or other analogous to Christ, the author of the Epistle to the Hebrews abundantly assures us. Besides his testimony, there is a remarkable fact which renders us certain not only of the analogy, but that there was some peculiarity in the work of Christ which rendered the continuance of sacrifices unnecessary, and even improper. I mean the universal concurrence of all who believe any portion of the Bible to abandon the rite. That Christ should accomplish this great religious revolution, the prophet Daniel foretold; (Dan. ix. 27;) and it must, therefore, have been distinctly determined in the divine counsels even before the absolute destruction of the Jewish nation and polity. God, by a strange and dreadful providence, fulfilled this prediction; and among all the effects of the famine during the siege of Jerusalem by the Roman armies, it is likely that few were more startling than the ceasing of the daily oblation.

It should be remarked, that sacrifices were no accidents of the Jewish system of religion. They were not partially required by it, but appear to enter into its very essence and heart. They were exceedingly numerous, and constantly repeated. The neglect of them was associated with the most severe penalties, and no duty was more pointedly stated or more urgently enforced. At once God ordains that they shall cease; that the whole system shall be swept away for ever. The most splendid temple in the world; the most venerable priesthood; the most complicated and costly system of sacrifice; all are suddenly blotted out from under heaven, never more to be restored; and it is worthy of remark, that the hand of God was as remarkably distinct in the destruction of the religious polity of the Jews, as his commandment in its origin. Nay, more; all the sacrificial obligations under which the Jews were laid, are as fully destroyed as the splendid structure under which they were recognised and discharged; and these obligations, it is universally admitted, are never to be restored.

Whatever may have been the reason for this amazing alteration in the religious aspect of the world, it is at least certain, that it was in one way or other immediately connected with the work of Christ. The question then naturally arises, what has Christ done, that the whole of the Jewish religion should be thus at once abrogated? The only reply that can be offered is, that he has effected all that the sacrifices of the law were designed to effect. He has done that at once which they were for many ages employed to do. He has so effectually accomplished his work, that no priesthood, no animal offering, no shedding of blood, will ever again be necessary. Were we, therefore, capable of doubting that text of Scripture to which we have before referred, historical facts would be distinctly demonstrative of the analogy.

You will perceive at once that this analogy is between the death of Christ and that of animal victims. There is no other circumstance upon which we can fix that admits of any rational comparison. And here we are naturally led to ask the rejecter of the atonement, whether the shedding of the blood of animals is one of those modes of worship which reason dictates. If he says, "Yes," he convicts himself of irrationality, because he has abandoned it; but if he says, "No," then he must for ever give up his reason as a test of religious truth, since he admits of a divine appointment, which reason does not teach or ordain. And if he allows that it was wise in God to appoint a series of sacrifices, although his reason would never have suggested this mode of divine worship, there is hope that he may ultimately be led to admit the same reasoning in the case of the atonement, and to grant that God might, with the most perfect wisdom and goodness, have ordained that Christ should be a vicarious sacrifice and propitiation for the sins of mankind.

If the foregoing reasoning be at all conclusive, you will admit that any theory upon the subject of ancient sacrifices which divests them of their analogical character, must be incorrect. And on the other hand, equally must those opinions be erroneous which represent the death of Christ as offering no analogy to those sacrifices which it superseded. If, for example, it is affirmed that the sacrifices of patriarchal and Mosaical times were only expressions of gratitude, it is certain, since the sufferings of Christ cannot be regarded in this light, that such an assertion is substantially untrue. And if it be said that the death of Christ was merely in attestation of the truths he taught, it is plain, since the sacrifices in question have no such character, that this opinion also is without foundation.

Besides, if animal sacrifices were merely designed as expressions of gratitude, there is no reason for their discontinuance, since the duty of testifying our sense of the divine goodness belongs to all time. Say that they are abrogated by the command of God, and you admit either that the purpose for which they were instituted is accomplished, or that they are unsuitable modes of eucharistic acknowledgment. The latter opinion will hardly be avowed, since it reflects upon the divine wisdom in their institution. It must, therefore, be admitted that they were but of temporary utility; and that their utility ceased upon the death of Christ.

Still further: it is to be remarked that Christians still possess a eucharistic symbol in the sacrament of the Lord's supper. Whatever was purely eucharistic, therefore, in ancient sacrifices is continued in that institution; but the sacrifices themselves were so totally different from it, that it cannot be rationally supposed that it can answer all the ends for which they were designed. It would seriously reflect upon the divine wisdom, to imagine that He commanded the immolation of millions of useful animals, and the consumption of their flesh by fire, when the same purpose might have been answered by the simple participation of bread and wine. The sacrament, which we denominate "the eucharist," is, also, a festival commemorative of the passion of Christ. This, of course, ancient sacrifices could not be; and even if it were granted that it was designed to occupy their place, it can only be by the admission that as it indicates Christ retrospectively, so they pointed to him prospectively; which is allowing a considerable part of the analogy for which we contend.

Now, if it be granted that the ancient sacrifices directed the attention of the Hebrews and their ancestors to Christ, and awoke their expectation, it must also be allowed that there was something in the work of Christ by which they were to be benefited. Otherwise, the whole system must have been, as far as they were concerned, without advantage or interest. Nothing, in short, could be more unprofitable, and, consequently, more irrational. We commemorate the death of Christ, because his work, both as a Prophet and as an atonement, has been of the highest profit to us. Our ordinance is, therefore, at once a memorial and a eucharist. It is, therefore, clear that there must have been in the sacrifices of the Old Testament something beyond a eucharistic design; and, in short, some object totally distinct from any existing usage in the Christian church.

Besides, only look at sacrifices and their alleged eucharistic intention. It is, perhaps, urged, that the devotion of our property to the service of God is a rational method of expressing our gratitude. So it is, beyond doubt; but the question is, whether the shedding of animal blood is so. If animals are to be devoted to God, it is certainly most natural that they should be preserved alive, and kept, as sacred herds were kept by some Heathens, far from other animals and from profane usage. But the fact is, that the devotion of animals at all to such a purpose, for the expression of gratitude merely, is exceedingly absurd. A man may be profited by such a gift; but surely it is most irrational to suppose that God can take any delight in the eucharistic devotion of a bullock or a goat. Were there any moral purposes supposed to be accomplished by any mode of conduct, it would not matter how comparatively trivial it might appear. But in the case before us, no moral purposes are alleged to have been entertained. The sacrifices are represented as acts for the expression of thankfulness, to which it is further supposed God gave tokens of his approbation. That is, he delighted in the destruction of innocent animals, independent of all moral results; and the shedding of blood was pleasing to Him whose tender mercies are over all his works.

Another supposition as to sacrifices is, that they partook of the nature of mulcts—a religion of fines! Daily fines, and annual fines; fines for individuals, and fines for the nation; fines for specific sin, and fines without any specific sin! This opinion, of course, cannot consist with the former. If they were judicial inflictions, they could not have been expressions of gratitude. But this notion is as absurd as the former. If sacrifices were fines for sins committed, there is no reason why they should have been discontinued, because sin is still committed, and, therefore, should still be mulcted in the same way. Was the death of Christ a mulct? If not, the sacrifices in question could not have been so. Otherwise the undeniable analogy would be destroyed.

Nothing can be more manifest than that sacrifices were religious ordinances; but to explain them as fines is wholly to secularize them, and to render them parts of a political government. And then, to impose a fine, absolutely and compulsorily, against which there was no appeal; to decree a punishment when there has been no proof of a sin; and to appoint that men should be subjected to it irrespective of all sin, as in the case of the daily oblation, is worse than unjust; and, far from producing any valuable effect, would be likely to beget a perfect indifference to the claims of the theocracy, and a most complete abhorrence to its yoke.

It is plain, therefore, that sacrifices were not fines, nor merely eucharistic appointments. It is equally plain that they were analogous to the death of Christ. But what was the nature of the analogy which subsisted between them? You will perceive, that, in this instance, we labour under a disadvantage unusual in analogical reasoning. The relation of one of the terms of the analogy is commonly ascertained and indisputable; and from what is known, we are readily able to argue upon what is not known. But here we have to dispute both parts of our analogy. If, however, the existence of the analogy is ascertainable, as I think I have shown it to be, we have escaped our only difficulty; since, when we have obtained satisfaction as to the nature of ancient sacrifices, the nature of the passion of Christ will be obvious, as a matter of course,

One of the most striking facts connected with the history of the Jewish religion, is the singular prominence given to the shedding of the blood of victims. To the mind of a devout Jew, therefore, the idea of religion must constantly have been associated with that of pain and death. The necessary result must have been, that his conceptions of the divine character would be of a very mixed order. Many things around him would suggest the notion of God's goodness; but the whole of the sacrificial system would tend to impress upon his mind, that there must be attributes in the divine nature widely different from the tender and endearing exhibitions of it, which the mind usually delights to contemplate. Independent of any supernatural communication on the subject, this, I think, would be likely to be his first impression.

A second impression which the sacrificial system would be likely to produce is, that, in one way or other, the shedding of blood was essential to a perfect system of religion. He would remark, that the nations around him, idolatrous as they were, still retained this rite; and, in fact, he could hardly have formed a conception of any sort of religion apart from it. It would not be difficult for him to combine these two conceptions, and to arrive at a third, namely, that the necessity for the effusion of blood arose from something in the nature of man, as contemplated by the sterner attributes of the divine character. He would have no difficulty in perceiving this to be sin. Nothing else in human nature could demand the operation of such attributes.

Apart from the distinct testimony of the Mosaic law, therefore, a pious Israelite, possessed of ordinary reflective powers, would be able to conclude, that it was the sin of man which rendered necessary the shedding of animal blood. The idea of substitution would unavoidably follow. He could not fail to perceive that God had ordained that, though it was right that man should be punished as a sinner, he, nevertheless, would accept the life of an animal instead of the actual destruction of the offender; and though perhaps he might have been at a loss to understand the grounds of this arrangement, yet, if he were duly impressed with the wisdom and righteousness of God, he would not fail to acquiesce in it as an arrangement at once justifiable and gracious.

I think, too, that such an individual could scarcely fail to have, occasionally at least, some suspicion of the imperfection of such vicarious sacrifices: their frequent repetition, their want of equivalency, either single or in the aggregate, the absence of everything like abstract fitness, would be very likely to suggest to him, independent of all immediately divine instruction, the probability of some more perfect institution of a sacrificial kind, which should possess the character of ample fitness, equivalency, and permanence. And if his mind had been enlightened as to the glory of "the world to come," he would have no difficulty in a specific allusion to it in all his speculations upon the subject.

It is highly probable, therefore, that a person under the Mosaic dispensation, even if he were without any distinct divine testimony, would, by a pious meditation upon the sacrificial system, arrive at the conclusion, that it was at once vicarious and analogical; or, to employ a more apposite word, typical. But, beyond all this, the direct testimony of the law itself, combined with all the forms employed in its sacrifices, would allow him to entertain no doubt as to their vicarious character. The statements of Scripture upon this subject I shall more immediately consider in my next letter.

Letter VI.

MY DEAR FRIEND,
THE FIRST SACRIFICE of which the Scriptures give us any account is that of Abel. The history of it is but cursory, and the exposition of it by the author of the Epistle to the Hebrews is short. Yet this latter, I believe, will be found sufficiently ample for our purpose. "By faith Abel offered unto God a more excellent sacrifice than Cain, by which he obtained witness that he was righteous, God testifying of his gifts: and by it he being dead yet speaketh." (Heb. xi. 4.) Upon the first glance at this passage, it is easy to perceive that in the sacrifice of Abel, its principle, and its result, is to be found a doctrine of universal and permanent importance: "by it he being dead yet speaketh." This, of course, would not have been announced, had the fact with which it stands connected been one of trivial or of transient interest. There is, indeed, a peculiar vividness in the phrase; and it appears to have been employed to arrest especial attention. But if the sacrifice of Abel be explained as merely eucharistic, or as the simple act of a virtuous man, without any further

or emphatic meaning, the statement becomes in the last degree vapid and trifling. It involves nothing but the very commonest truth, and displays no more than we naturally expect from every well-disposed mind. It is impossible, therefore, to avoid the conclusion, that more, much more, is intended, than any such exposition of the passage would involve.

Abel's sacrifice was that of an animal victim, and it was offered by faith: not, observe, by gratitude, nor by the mere exercise of his rational powers, but by faith. Now, faith is explained, in the first verse of the same chapter, and in close connexion with this passage, as the evidence of things not seen," &c. Of course, faith must, in all cases, have respect to some divine communication. He, however, would possess a very partial and incorrect view of faith in general, who should attribute to it only an apprehension of truths which natural reason is capable of discovering; and in the faith of Abel there can be no doubt that there was a certain eminence which peculiarly demands our attention. Faith, in its most common scriptural acceptation, respects the promise of God, "things hoped for," of which it substantially assures. It cannot be denied, therefore, that Abel's sacrifice was of divine appointment, or it would not have been of faith. It equally appears, that it respected some good to be obtained, or it would not have been a thing hoped for. What, then, was the advantage? Clearly, the justification of his person. By it "he obtained witness that he was righteous."

Here, then, is the first of animal sacrifices ordained by God, and procuring the pardon of him that offered it, because offered in faith, steadfast trust, upon Him that had so promised. But even this does not reach the whole of the case. The only promise of which the Bible gives us any account, before the transaction in question, was a promise of the seed of the woman, and his hostility to the seed of the serpent, through which he was himself at first to be a sufferer, but ultimately a complete victor. That the terms of this promise are mysterious, will be readily admitted; but that Abel understood its real meaning, seems all but demonstrable from the fact, that upon this ground alone he offered a sacrifice for obtaining the pardon of sin.

There is also a peculiarity in the terms employed in describing the blessing which the faith of Abel succeeded in procuring. Not only was he righteous; not merely did his reliance upon the promise of God, and his consequent sacrifice, ensure his justification; but, as if God would show a peculiar and emphatic approbation of his spirit and conduct, it is added, *"he obtained witness* that he was righteous." He received the divine assurance to this effect, and to all ages secured the divine testimony. Hence, by our Lord himself, he is called "righteous Abel;" and St. John supplies a similar statement. Thus is his sacrifice presented to the continual observation of pious minds, especially in its prevalence.

Beyond this, it has the advantage of contrast to render it yet more impressive. He offered a more acceptable sacrifice than Cain. If Abel's offering was rendered acceptable to God by faith, in his brother the absence of faith must have been the cause of his rejection. There may have been other causes combined with this; but we have nothing specific to this effect in Scripture. Now, Cain's unbelief operated in inducing him to offer to God a sacrifice of fruits; and had this act of the first brothers been merely eucharistic, I confess that, in my judgment, the elder would have had the advantage. Upon the rejection of Cain's sacrifice, God condescended to reason with him: "If thou doest well, shalt thou not be accepted? and if thou doest not well, sin lieth at the door." (Gen. iv. 7.) The doing well here undoubtedly refers to the sacrifice in question, as there is no previous transaction in the life of Cain of which we have the slightest hint; and it cannot be supposed that the divine expostulation would have thus been placed in such peculiar prominence, if we had been left wholly unacquainted with the reasons upon which it was founded. And it must, therefore, be to this that St. John refers, when he says that the works of Cain were evil; because, except this, we have no part of Cain's history before the murder of his brother; which flagitious act the Apostle refers to the hatred conceived by him against his brother, in consequence of the contrast between their conduct. The drift of the divine reasoning with Cain was this, If he did well, and offered up a suitable sacrifice, he should most certainly be accepted, not his offering merely, but himself also; while, if he did not well, the fault was his own, and consequently he had no one but himself to blame for his rejection. Does not this, then, most distinctly imply, that God had given every needful instruction as to the nature and design of sacrifice? A departure from a prescribed mode would certainly incur guilt; but a mere error in judgment, where there was no adequate source of information, would not have been thus denounced. Cain must have known that God had chosen to be propitiated by the shedding of blood; and because he did not acknowledge the divine appointment, he and his sacrifice were rejected.

In the conduct of Abel we find a recognition of that great analogy which we are solicitous to establish. The promise of the Redeemer supplied the first impulse to his faith: the justification of his person through an analogical rite was its proximate object. Whether Abel understood all the circumstances which gave emphasis and force to the type of his own sacrifice, it is not now needful to inquire. That he had sufficient information for every practical purpose, will not be matter of dispute.

But whether Abel had or had not a clear discovery of all the points of analogy between the shedding of the blood of an animal, and the conflict of the seed of the woman, it is certain that such an analogy existed. Otherwise, faith in the first promise would not have led to a sacrifice, and there was no other promise of which we have any information. In the mind of God, therefore, there must have been a determination to institute this analogy for the instruction of all subsequent ages; and hence he gave peculiar publicity (so to speak) to the first practical acknowledgment of its existence. It is natural, therefore, for us to inquire into the meaning of the sacrifice of Abel, in connexion with the fulfilment of that first promise upon which his faith was founded.

The penalty of sin was death. This Abel knew. He knew also that this penalty had not yet been inflicted upon his parents, who had sinned, nor upon their sinful posterity, of whom he was one. He causes an animal to die, and hereupon is himself pardoned. Nothing could be more plain than the notion of transfer and substitution involved in this act. It is admitted, that by the bruising of the heel of the promised seed, is intended the triumph of death over Christ's mortal nature; and by the bruising of the serpent's head, the triumph of Christ over the various spiritual ills which afflict mankind. In this sense, with more or less clearness, Abel must have understood this promise. The blessing which he obtains is a deliverance from the penalty of sin, and this he must therefore have contemplated in the bruising of the serpent's head. The immediate cause of this blessing to himself, was the effusion of the blood of an animal. He must, therefore, have considered the bruising of the heel as signifying suffering, unmerited, indeed, by the seed of the woman, but suffering which partook, in one degree or other, of the nature of a transferred penalty; and suffering which should necessarily precede and induce the bestowment of the highest blessings upon man. Less than this we cannot conceive sufficient to generate a faith The one so operative as that of Abel; and more is not needful to the argument.

One word more, and I dismiss the subject. It is easy, with these views, to perceive the reason why Abel's sacrifice was more acceptable than that of Cain. In the one, there was an admission of the guilt of sin: the other was entirely destitute of any thing resembling such an admission. In this, there was a reference to the illustrious subject of the first promise: in that, there was a complete absence of any such allusion. Cain's offering was a gift; Abel's a sacrifice. The one assumed the posture of an innocent person rendering merely an acknowledgment of God as the Creator: the other presented himself as a sinner, with his substitution in his hand, the blood of which he shed, by faith in that divine provision for human guilt, of which the firstling of his flock was an emblem. This view of the subject, you will admit, relieves it from all difficulty; and nothing could be more fitting than that God should have honoured the faith of Abel. But, abandon this mode of exposition, and I am utterly at a loss to conceive how you will succeed in explaining this interesting subject. Previous to the murder of Abel, the era of which we do not know, we have no sort of information of the moral character of the two first-born of men, beyond that comprised in the history of their respective sacrifices; and upon the facts of this history, and the fair deductions to be made from it, our opinions are to be formed. With this caution, I think I may now leave the subject to your consideration.

Of the religious rites pertaining to the Noahic theology, our information, as directly bearing on the subject of sacrifice, is even less than that which we possess respecting the offering of Abel. The fact that sacrifices formed a part of the religious worship of Noah and his immediate posterity, is not questioned; but it is only by inference that we can ascertain the peculiarities connected with them. There are, however, two circumstances which it is proper to notice. The first is, the distinction between clean and unclean beasts; the second, the obligation to abstain from blood. The one is principally important, as a proof of the divine origin of sacrifices; and upon this subject it is certainly very satisfactory. The animals appointed to sacrificial services were thus distinctly designated by God. Of these a perfect number of pairs (seven) was to be preserved in the ark; while of other animals only two were so to be secured. Apart from religious considerations, there is no rational method of accounting for this distinction; and it is to be remarked, as an evidence of the prevalence of sacrifices before the flood, that this distinction was understood by Noah; and the manner in which the terms are employed, evinces that they were of popular use and distinct significance. And, on the other hand, the employment of them by God is the most satisfactory sanction of their ordinary use, and an evidence that the distinction implied in them had originated with himself.

The command of God that blood should be abstained from, is attributed to three different causes. By some it is supposed to have been designed as a preventive to the cruel custom of employing for food portions of a living animal. The principal objection to this opinion is, that it is perfectly gratuitous. There is no sort of evidence that animal food was used at all before the flood. In fact, every probability is opposed to such a supposition. It could not, therefore, have been necessary to forbid the eating of blood, upon the ground of any such custom as the one under consideration. Indeed, there is no evidence that it has ever prevailed in any nation. A few solitary instances of such barbarity there undoubtedly have been; but that any express commandment for its prevention should have been necessary among the few precepts granted to Noah and his immediate posterity, merely on such grounds, is altogether improbable. Besides, if it were proper to guard against cruelty to the brute creation, why does this prohibition thus stand alone? Why is not the impropriety of all cruelty specifically stated? or why are not other instances of it specified and forbidden? The fact is notorious, indeed, that this precept, in its application to the Israelites, was not applied to eating part of a living animal, but to eating the flesh of any dead animal which had not been slain by the effusion of blood; and this is conclusive against the opinion in question.

A second mode of accounting for this precept is by the supposition that it was designed to prevent the sons of Noah from partaking unhealthy food, such as blood is supposed to be. But this is equally gratuitous with the foregoing theory. In addition, it is also to be remarked, that such an opinion is confuted by the entire tenor of the passage of which the command to abstinence from blood forms a part. "Every moving thing that liveth shall be meat for you." Here, you remark, there is no sort of restriction as to healthy or unhealthy food. The qualities of food in general, with their various degrees of suitableness to the human appetite and constitution, were to be matters of experiment. But had it been the design of God to prevent the use of unsuitable meat, the obvious course would have been a distinct statement of those animals whose flesh was improper to be eaten. But, this not having been done, it is clear that the divine intention was not such as this opinion supposes. In fact, it may be questioned whether blood is unhealthy food in any peculiar sense; and, in the absence of evidence of that fact, we may safely pronounce this theory as untenable as the former.

There is, indeed, all the evidence which we can desire

that the ground on which the use of blood was forbidden was principally, if not exclusively, religious. I do not know whether you place any confidence in the alleged tradition of what are called the seven precepts of Noah. For myself, I confess that I do not; but there are certain admirers of what is called natural religion who are accustomed to refer to them with considerable emphasis. On this ground, therefore, I refer to them here. You will readily perceive, in glancing over them, that six of them are exclusively religious and moral. The seventh enforces the abstinence from blood. The natural conclusion, therefore, is, that this also partook of the same character. But upon this it is not needful to insist. The Levitical law, however, is more explicit upon the subject. In two places, the prohibition of blood is accompanied by that of the fat of animals actually slain; (Levit. iii. 17; viii. 23-27;) and this is most decisive against the opinion that the blood of living animals is that meant in the Noahic precept. Indeed, the reason of the prohibition is most explicitly stated. The fat and the blood were sacred; and upon this ground alone can we reconcile the severity of the law upon this subject with the divine equity. He that transgressed it was to be cut off; but surely it is irrational to suppose that such a punishment was to be inflicted because a person partook of unhealthy food. There must have been, as indeed it is demonstrable that there actually was, a religious reason for the severity of such an ordinance. That reason is stated Levit. xvii. 10-14, a passage which, as I shall hereafter have occasion to show, states the doctrine of expiation by the effusion of blood as explicitly as language can possibly convey it. If, then, God had appointed the blood of animals for so important a purpose of religion, there was every reason why the ordinary or profane use of it should be forbidden. This was accordingly the case, even with Noah and his immediate descendants. And when a reason so weighty is supplied by Scripture itself, for a prohibition which otherwise might appear arbitrary or trifling, there is no necessity for further inquiry.

If any objection to this view should suggest itself to your mind from the cursory way in which the subject is treated, I beg to recall to your recollection that Moses was writing primarily for the Israelites, who had the most ample commentary upon it in their own rites and their own law; while for those who should afterwards possess the whole of the Pentateuch, there was no more reason for any detail than in the case of the Israelites themselves. Yet it does not by any means follow, that the communication to Noah, upon the unlawfulness of eating blood, was restricted to the single sentence which has been handed down to us. It is not credible that we have, in the book of Genesis, an account of all, or even of most, of the communications made by God to men. We have only such as it is important that we should know; and when Moses had to compress within a few pages the history of considerably more than two thousand years, it was necessary that his account, even of these, should be exceedingly cursory.

It is not, therefore, at all probable that the Noahic prohibition of the eating of blood should have been unaccompanied by some reason, unless we suppose, what is very likely, that Noah was so conversant with the doctrine of expiation by the effusion of animal blood, as to render any such communication unnecessary. You will be better able to judge upon the subject, by reading attentively the first part of Gen. ix. Here you will remark, that the sacredness of human life is distinctly accounted for: man was made in the image of God; and therefore the shedding of human blood was high treason against the divine vicegerent. This was probably an entirely new view of the reason for reverence to human life. It is no rash conjecture, that the guilt of murder had, before the flood, been inferred, from the relation of man to his fellow. "And the Lord said unto Cain, The voice of thy brother's blood crieth unto me from the ground. And now art thou cursed from the earth," &c. "And Cain said unto the Lord, Behold, thou hast driven me out this day from the earth; and from thy face shall I be hid; and I shall be a fugitive and a vagabond in the earth; and it shall come to pass, that every one that findeth me shall slay me." (Gen. iv. 9-14.) It was proper, therefore, that this additional protection should be cast round the human person, by giving a new and more fearful character to the crime of murder. A reason for the other prohibition was equally unnecessary, except upon the foregoing supposition.

It perhaps may occur to you to inquire, if the doctrine of expiation by the shedding of blood be so important as to render necessary the prohibition of a profane use of blood in any case, how did it happen that it was not given till after the flood? To this I reply, that it was not till after the flood that the use of animal food was granted by God. All animals lawfully slain before were therefore sacrifices. Of course, this prohibition was not then needful, since the whole of the animal was sacred. But now that men were, for the first time, permitted to employ animals for ordinary food, it was necessary that they should be reminded, that though flesh might lawfully be eaten, there was still a part of every animal to be separated from all profane uses; and this was the life-the blood. The practical result of this you will instantly perceive. It was a universal admonition, that the divine claims extended not merely to ordinary obedience, but to the forfeiture of life itself on account of transgression. No pious and enlightened Patriarch could forget the relation in which he stood to God as a sinner, when his daily food was accompanied by an abstinence so significant. On the other hand, he would constantly see reason to adore the divine goodness, which thus permitted him to enjoy the blessings of Providence on a condition so easy, and mingled so large a proportion of mercy with the impressive memorial of justice.

Letter VII.

My dear Friend,

In my last Letter I endeavoured to prove, that expiation by the shedding of blood was, in the patriarchal age, appointed by God, and understood by the pious. We come now, more particularly, to consider this doctrine recognised among the Israelites, under the Levitical dispensation. And here I think you will find the subject more clear than before, and the evidence as ample as the nature of the case will admit.

Some of the errors which have obtained in the church, upon the subject of the Jewish rite, may possibly be attributable to a want of distinct classification. There are two sorts of ordinances in the Levitical economy. The one respects God as the head of the theocracy; and the other, as the great moral governor of the universe. Certain sin and trespass offerings belonged to the former class; burnt-offerings generally, peace-offerings, and some others, to the latter. Yet there are so many respects in which they possessed a common character, that some of the reasoning applicable to one is also suited to the other; and inferences suggested by the latter are not unfrequently to be equally deduced from the former. The sacrificial rites, of a religious character, are also capable of distinct classification. Some of them were primarily eucharistic; while others are unintelligible, except upon the admission of their expiatory efficacy. These last certainly hold the most prominent place in the Jewish ceremonial.

The distinction to which I have just adverted appears to be recognised by the author of the Epistle to the Hebrews, where he says, that "every High-Priest is ordained to offer gifts" (δωρα) "and sacrifices" (θυσιας). That these terms are sometimes employed indifferently by the version of the Seventy, and by the writers of the New Testament, will not be denied; but it is, I think, equally clear, that some offerings may, with peculiar propriety, be distinguished as gifts, and others as sacrifices; and you have perhaps remarked, that I have already ventured to use these distinctive terms in reference to the respective offerings of Cain and Abel. With the former of these terms we have not so much concern in our present argument. I propose to confine my remarks to those offerings which were emphatically "sacrifices."

The term which is employed by the Seventy, and by the writers of the New Testament, (θυσια,) suggests to us an important view of these rites. For θυσια not only signifies the victim immolated, but, properly and primarily, the act of immolation. This is evident upon the first glance at its derivation. Θυω is "to slay;" and the actual slaying of a victim is therefore called θυσια. Now, this admirably corresponds with the real facts of Jewish sacrifices. It is true that the holocaust was not complete till the victim was consumed upon the altar; but it is equally true that the shedding of its blood was the peculiarly significant part of the ordinance. Thus, θυσια is distinguished from προσφορα, the simple presentation of a victim; (Psal. xl. 6; Heb. x. 5;) from σφαγιον, a slain animal in general; (Amos v. 25, 26; Acts vii. 42;) or a free-will offering, as it is once used by the Seventy; (Levit. xxii. 23;) and from ολοκαυτωμα, the actual holocaust. (Mark xii. 33.) This term is employed in several hundred instances by the Seventy, and not unfrequently in the New Testament; and there is not one that could have been chosen which would more accurately have expressed that peculiarity in sacrifice which we are concerned to advocate.

How admirably, for example, does it harmonize with the remarkable passage in Levit. xvii., to which I have already alluded, and to which it will be proper here to direct your attention more fully: "The life of the flesh is in the blood, and I have given it you upon the altar to make an atonement for your souls: for it is the blood that maketh an atonement for the soul." (Ver. 11.) This passage is given substantially in the same sense by all the ancient versions. The word נפש *nephesh,* which is rendered "life," in the former part, is twice translated "soul" in the latter; and the same uniformity of phrase is preserved in the most ancient versions. Some of them read, "The life or soul of all flesh is in the blood;" and this explains the word "flesh" as signifying, what it often elsewhere means, all animals possessing a sensitive life. The passage, therefore, may thus be paraphrased: "The sensitive soul of all living beings is in the blood; and the blood or life of beasts offered in sacrifice I have given to make, by sacrificial death, a propitiation for your souls; for it is by the shedding of blood, the effusion of the life, that a propitiation is made for the soul." Nothing, surely, can more clearly convey the notion of transfer and substitution. The *nephesh* of the sacrifice is instead of the *nephesh* of the offerer; and because this *nephesh* is in the blood, therefore blood was sacred from ordinary uses. The life of the victim was the appointed means by which propitiation was to be made for the life of man. Life for life, soul for soul, the sacrifice for the sacrificer.

The primary, or, as some critics call it, the formal, signification of the word כפר *copher*, here rendered "atonement," is "to cover:" hence the mercy-seat, which covered the ark of the covenant, is expressed by it. Now as the cover of anything conceals from the eye all that is beneath it, so is the life of the victim, in the passage before us, represented as covering the soul from the stroke of divine justice. The blood interposes between God and the sinner, as a surety between a judge and a criminal, or a substitute between the executioner and the convict. The soul is given as a covering for the soul. Then, in continuation of the same meaning, the word is employed to signify that which propitiates, renders a being not only placable, but actually complacent towards another. This is its regular acceptation when applied to the Levitical rites; and here I cannot but remark, that it perfectly corresponds with the Greek word, $\iota\lambda\alpha\sigma\kappa\omega$, or $\iota\lambda\alpha\sigma\kappa o\mu\alpha\iota$ (two Greek words missing), which, with its derivatives, is used by the LXX. for its translation; and this is the very word employed by New Testament writers to Christ. "He is the propitiation for our sins." As the shedding of blood under the law was that which interposed between God and him who offered the sacrifice, and as it propitiated the Governor of the universe, even so Christ comes between sinful man and the Father, and hence is called the Mediator. Even so does he, by the infinite virtue of his blood, render God complacent toward the sinner, who otherwise must have stood exposed, in the naked deformity of his transgressions, to the just infliction of the punishment of a violated law. Here, therefore, you will perceive, in both cases, is the notion of substitution, intervention, and propitiation; and these render the analogy as complete as we are capable of conceiving it.

Observe how fully this doctrine pervades the Jewish rites. It was required that a propitiation should be made, not merely for the people, but for the tabernacle and the instruments of religious worship. God, in effect, refused to look with complacency upon any thing which had been touched by the hand of man, except so far as it was purified by the sprinkling of blood. No part even of inanimate substances could be employed for religious purposes, except there was connected with it the recognition of the great doctrine under consideration. Every thing must present the memorial of man's sinfulness, and of the only method of salvation by a transferred penalty and a substituted victim. The principle was to be preserved even in eucharistic acts, and in many of the civil rites, as well as in those more particularly tending to expiation, and the doctrine that it is blood which makes atonement for the life, extended to ordinary food and the daily habits of men.

It may, I think, be safely affirmed, that no system could be more fully saturated, if I may so speak, with the memorials of expiation by blood than that of the Israelites; but while this principle presented itself on every hand, there were certain rites to which its exposition peculiarly belonged, and to which it was, in a great degree, indebted for its impressiveness. To these I may briefly direct your particular attention.

The first of these is the daily oblation. In Exod. xxix. 38-42, you will find an account of this ordinance. The design of it appears to be twofold: to effect a daily propitiation, and to supply evidence of the constant complacent regard of God to his people. It is not difficult to perceive how such an institution was likely to operate. To the mind of a pious Hebrew, it would represent the necessity of a constant reference to the great doctrine which it taught. It would teach him, that the favourable regard of God was to be obtained only by a perpetual substitution, and that no single day could be blessed, except so far as it was hallowed by the shedding of blood. Upon this were to be founded all those religious emotions which are of the more agreeable kind: the tokens of the divine favour were obviously its result: and thus were taught, at once, reverence for the divine character, and gratitude for divine benefits.

But a still more impressive rite was that of the animal expiation, — a service the avowed and sole object of which was the acknowledgment of transgression, and propitiation for it. The day appointed for it was wholly consecrated to religious engagements: it was a Sabbath of rest. It was also a season of peculiar humiliation: they were "to afflict their souls by a statute for ever." The approach of the High-Priest to God was according to prescribed mode, under pain of death. He bathed his whole person, to indicate the spiritual qualifications needful for his duty; and then he put on the full dress of his office. First he killed a bullock, in behalf of himself and his family; and having in his hand a censer full of sacred fire, he entered into the immediate presence of God, sprinkling incense on the censer, and sending up a cloud of perfume between the cherubim. He then sprinkled the blood of his own sin-offering before the mercy-seat; and having thus made a propitiation for himself, proceeded to perform similar rites for the people. Meantime the congregation remained at a distance, not even coming into the ordinary place of their worship, but waiting till the solemnities of the holiest place were completed. Two goats had been previously chosen for this service, one of which had been appointed by lot to die. Its blood was sprinkled before the Lord, as that of the bullock had been sprinkled before. Still further, this propitiatory service was extended to the tabernacle and altar. The blood of the bullock and of the goat was sprinkled as before, and thus the place was purified from the pollution which it had contracted from the sins of the worshippers.

A peculiarly significant part of the service yet remained to be performed. The High-Priest now took the living goat, and laying his hands upon its head, in this position confessed the transgressions of the children of Israel; and thus, by the most emphatic of symbols, represented the transfer of guilt. The animal, "bearing upon him all the iniquities of the people," was then committed to the care of a suitable person, who took him into some solitary and desert spot, and let him go. After this part of the service, the sacrifice was completed by the burnt-offering of the slain animals. That which was not placed upon the altar was consumed by fire without the camp; and the Priest, the person who led the goat into the wilderness, and he who burnt the remains of the sin-offerings, washed themselves from the pollution contracted in the several acts which they had thus performed. Thus terminated this most impressive rite; of which it may be safely said, that a more vivid representation of the doctrine now under consideration could not have been conceived. Here is contrition, propitiation, confession, the transfer of guilt, and the bearing it away; and each brought out with such distinctness and particularity, as to preclude the confusion of ideas, and all probability of mistake.

Now, these two rites, you will perceive, were made of perpetual obligation, irrespective of any peculiarity of guilt in the Israelites, and totally distinct from those sacrifices which were appointed for specific offences. No temporary moral condition, nor anything of a contingent nature, was to render these duties more or less imperative. The government of God demanded an uninterrupted admission of human guilt, and a constant recognition of expiation by the effusion of blood. The afflicting of the soul on the day of expiation fully proves that it was not an eucharistic appointment; while the unvarying character of the obligation to observe it, as fully decides that it partook in no degree of the nature of a mulct. Nothing but the unchangeable relation of man to God could justify the continuation of these rites; and thus, on every hand, we are compelled to the conclusion, that our sinful race can only become acceptable to God by the transfer of our deserved penalty to a vicarious victim.

There are several other parts of the Levitical economy to which I should like to allude, were I not afraid of swelling my letter to an undue size. The law of leprosy you will find very significant. The paschal rites are also highly instructive. The redemption of the first-born males possesses features of considerable interest; and several ceremonial purifications are fraught with meaning. It is not needful to the argument that I notice them at length; and I therefore content myself with a simple reference to them, that I may immediately resume the argument.

Analogical reasoning is often exceedingly erroneous. The state of science before the age of Lord Bacon, and the introduction of the inductive philosophy, supply the most satisfactory argument against its ordinary employment. But in the case now under consideration we are effectually secured against error in any conclusions which we may draw from analogy, and that for this simple reason: The designs of God in his moral government are uniform; and whatever varieties may mark the objects of scientific theory, there are none in the essential principles of the divine administration. It is this which gives a force and conclusiveness to all Scripture analogies. Thus it is demonstrable that if it was ever, in a single instance, the design of God to justify a sinner by the effusion of blood, no one can be pardoned in any other way. In that case this method must be invariable and unchangeable, applicable to all mankind, in all generations, even to the end of time. If, therefore, the preceding reasoning be conclusive, it is impossible not to perceive that this mode of propitiation and salvation is the only one which God ever has propounded, or ever will propound. The infinite perfections of God are involved in it: and he can as soon cease to be, as repeal their constitution. We cannot lay too much stress on the argument before us, since whatever are the conclusions to which it brings us, they are equally and for ever deducible from every other form which the divine administration may assume.

In ordinary analogy the terms may be, and often are, equivalent. I mean to say, that analogous objects may be equal in their importance; or the character of the being or thing to be ascertained may be even of less moment than that which we understand. But there is a species of analogy which, for the sake of perspicuity, I may call "symbolical analogy," in which the object known is invariably of smaller importance than that to be ascertained. The analogies of Scripture are generally of this kind; and by them God condescends to instruct us in the relations of spiritual things from those of sensible objects. The analogy between the sacrificial rites of the Jews and the work of Christ, you will perceive, is symbolical. But so far as an object symbolized transcends in importance the symbol by which its relations are described, so far is the work of Christ superior in interest and moment to the rites of the Jewish ceremonial. Yet even this hardly gives a sufficient view of the case. The analogy in question is not an accidental resemblance, but the subject of distinct appointment. The rites of the Israelites did not merely resemble the work of Christ, but were arranged for this express purpose; and every other design, real or supposed, was in them only secondary. Apart from this, they were in reality of no importance; for it was impossible that the blood of bulls and of goats could take away sin. This constitutes that species of symbolical analogy which the Scriptures describe by the term TYPE: and it is to be remarked as partaking in a very impressive degree of the nature of prophecy. Its principal characteristic, however, as distinguished from every other sort of analogy, is its exclusiveness. It belongs to the thing typified, and to it alone. It illustrates the nature of its antitype, and of it alone. To employ the striking phrase of the New Testament, it is a shadow, and, as a shadow, corresponds exactly to the substance which occasions it, and is not to be produced by any other body; even thus do the typical ordinances of Judaism describe, by adumbration, the passion and expiatory nature of him who is the body, even Christ.

Now, if an ordinary analogy is sufficient to indicate the unchangeable constitution of the divine government, it is certain that typical analogy is still more illustrative, and is indeed irresistible in its influence upon an enlightened mind. Because, if I may employ the expression, this is God's express bond, and he thus, in the face of mankind, lays himself under an acknowledged and understood obligation. It is a perpetual prophecy; a prophecy repeated every morning and evening, and renewed annually in the most solemn forms. An instructed Israelite found it in his daily food, and his continual intercourse with society. The civil polity under which he lived breathed the same spirit; and it was impossible for him to open his eyes without seeing a seal of that covenant by which God had bound himself to bless mankind with pardon and favour, through the shedding of the blood of Christ. I feel myself utterly unable to clothe this subject with its proper impressiveness. I wish I could only convey to your mind the emphasis and force with which it appeals to my own. Let me beg your most serious meditation upon it; and, unless I am greatly in error, you will not fail to perceive the infinite certainty of the great doctrine of the atonement of Christ.

Letter VIII.

MY DEAR FRIEND,

THE SUBSTITUTION OF the innocent for the guilty has been frequently objected to, as involving a breach of equity; and hence it has been argued, the doctrine of the atonement cannot be divine, because, in its very principle, it cannot consist with the infinite rectitude of God's nature and government. This is a mode of reasoning so specious, that it requires our particular attention; since nothing can be more certain, than that if this doctrine is irreconcilably at variance with the perfection of Deity, it is utterly untenable.

It is in reply to this objection that I have to beg your consideration of the second branch of analogical reasoning, to which I have already referred; namely, that supplied by the acknowledged and undeniable facts of the divine administration. I shall take it for granted that God exercises a government over all his creatures: I shall also assume that this government is conducted upon fixed and unchangeable principles, because any other supposition is at variance with the divine perfections. There is no law more obviously true, and more certainly equitable, than that which determines that piety and virtue shall ensure happiness, and that vice shall be attended by misery. Thus far, I presume, we are perfectly agreed. Now, whatever apparent variations from this law we may detect in the present order of things, it is nevertheless certain, that all the dispositions of the divine conduct are perfectly reconcilable with it; and whatever difficulties we may have in the attempt to reconcile them, they must arise from our own imperfection of knowledge, and will ultimately be most completely dissipated in that perfect state of knowledge and blessedness, which is the inheritance of the saints.

But the fact is, that, in the present state, prosperity is so far from being uniformly the attendant of piety, that, for the most part, the best of men are subjected to many inconveniences and sufferings. I am not now about to assign any reasons for this arrangement. Its existence is indisputable, and its propriety is therefore demonstrable. Hence it follows, as a general principle, that in this life it is not necessary that good and evil should be apportioned according to our notions of moral fitness. It is also equally clear that those notions are not adequate to decide upon the harmony of any doctrine with the plans of God's government; and that its being irreconcilable with them is no proof of its fallacy, but that, in many instances, this very fact, by its analogy with what we constantly witness, may supply a strong presumption in its favour.

To go a little more into detail. It is admitted on all hands that, on the whole, man's connexion with society is an incalculable good; and, consequently, that its appointment is not only righteous, but in the highest degree benevolent. Yet nothing is more common than for the crimes or follies of one man to affect the welfare of others, and that to an extreme degree. The inordinate ambition of a Monarch may multiply miseries to millions of men, and extend its destructive influence over the destinies of posterity for many ages. One sinner may entail disease, and poverty, and shame upon his descendants for many generations, and that without any fault of theirs, or any power of shunning these evils. By the constitution of social life, therefore, it is essentially impossible that happiness and misery should attend those individuals only whose virtues or crimes appear to merit them.

The disposition of the ranks of society necessarily involves the majority of men, irrespective of moral considerations, in circumstances of comparative inconvenience, and subjects a large proportion to considerable privation and suffering. Yet this variety of condition is unavoidably the result of an arrangement which must be admitted as highly equitable. It follows, therefore, that it consists with the most perfect justice that the greater part of mankind should be more or less subjected to natural evil, for the advantage of the remainder.

Nor do we find any regular deviation from this disposition of human affairs, in those visitations of calamity which the Bible represents as proceeding immediately from the hand of God. Thus, to Israel Jehovah says, "Behold, I am against thee, and will cut off from thee the righteous and the wicked," &c. (Ezek. xxi. 3, 4.) Nay, more: we are taught that it is an equitable method of punishment for the crime of an individual, that multitudes of others should be destroyed, while he himself is personally unhurt. The history of David's pestilence may be cited in illustration and proof. God proposed to his choice three modes of punishment for his sin, each of which did not affect himself, except by reflection; while each involved the destruction of many of his subjects. Defeat in war, famine, or pestilence, was offered to him; and the result of his choice was, that seventy thousand persons were slain by the immediate infliction of God.

The history of Joseph is still more applicable to our present argument. The atrocious wickedness of his brethren; the lewdness of his mistress; the ingratitude of his friend, led him, through slavery and protracted imprisonment, to the second place in Egypt. Had the record of his history terminated with the account of the forgetfulness of Pharaoh's butler, we might have been at a loss how to reconcile it with the rectitude of the divine character; but with the account of his subsequent elevation before us, all is clear and intelligible. The innocent man suffers, that he may by this very means attain that political influence which shall enable him to minister to the advantage of multitudes of vicious as well as reputable persons; and, among others, of those very individuals with whom his sufferings originated. And this interesting fact the pious Patriarch himself distinctly notices: "God," says he, "sent me before you to preserve you a posterity in the earth, and to save your lives by a great deliverance." Were it not anticipating the argument, I might here remark on the striking analogy between this eminent person and Him who, in his last hours, prayed, "Father, forgive them; for they know not what they do." But this I shall have occasion to advert to hereafter. One thing at least is certain, that if the history of Joseph presents no deviation from the equity of the divine government, the doctrine of the atonement is still more free from this ground of objection. The great principle, however, which I wish to impress upon your mind is, that it is not unjust to appoint the innocent, in the present state, to suffer with the guilty instead of the guilty, and for the advantage of the guilty.

All this, indeed, the Socinian scheme allows; and so far do its admissions proceed, as to enable us to turn this very argument against itself: for if it can be proved that the alleged reason for appointing an innocent man to suffer is insufficient to vindicate the divine equity, it is clear that such a reason is incorrect. The Socinian admits that Christ did suffer; that his sufferings were matters of distinct appointment by God; and that they were intended for the benefit of man. These facts are all so plainly revealed in the Bible, that he who denies them must wholly reject it. Now it is clear that God would not have subjected the most virtuous man that ever lived to extreme suffering; that he would not have represented this suffering as absolutely necessary; that he would not have awakened the expectation of men to these facts, by many prophecies uttered hundreds of years before their occurrence; that he would not have referred to the evils which Christ endured as productive of the highest good to man; and, in short, that he would not have represented them as surpassing in value every other sort of suffering, except for some very weighty reason; except, indeed, the benefits which should from them accrue to man, were far beyond the advantage which men might derive from all other sufferings which the world ever witnessed.

Now what is the Socinian theory on the subject of Christ's suffering? "He was a martyr," we are told. So was St. Stephen; but we are never said to be redeemed by him. So were St. Paul, St. Peter, and all the Apostles, except John; but we have not even an allusion to their martyrdom in the Bible, except in one instance. "He died to attest the truth of the doctrines he taught." So did they: but they were never the subjects of prophecy; their deaths are never said to have been necessary to the salvation of men; and the fact of their having sealed the truth with their blood is not even affirmed in the Bible. Christ was a great Prophet, the founder of a new system; and therefore his death was essential to its proper authentication." So was Moses; yet his death was not necessary. "But Christ died to supply us with an example of virtue, patience, heroism, and resignation, surpassing that of any other virtuous person." Then it may be safely said that this purpose was not accomplished. The death of Christ was not such an example. It was an infliction from which he shrank, and in the prospect of which his mind was overwhelmed with unutterable anguish. The heroic Ignatius courted the wreaths of martyrdom. But Christ would fain have avoided the pain of the cross, and cried, in his amazement and sorrow, "If it be possible, let this cup pass from me." (Matt. xxvi. 39.) You will perceive, therefore, that upon the Socinian scheme there was no eminence in the sufferings of Christ, no necessity for them, no example supplied by them, but what was excelled by those of others; and, in short, no peculiar advantage resulting from them. Hence it may be safely concluded that upon these principles they were utterly irreconcilable with the divine equity. I need not tell you what is the unavoidable inference.

The doctrine of the substitution of the innocent for the guilty, as illustrated in the sufferings of Christ, has often struck me as a subject of peculiar and extraordinary interest; and, if it be agreeable to you, I shall feel much pleasure in offering some remarks upon it in my subsequent communications. You will probably recollect that in the early part of our correspondence I proposed to treat of the atonement under three separate heads. The two first—necessity and analogy—I have now brought before you. It remains for me to speak on the third,—harmony; and this, as I have just intimated, I shall first endeavour to do in special reference to the vicarious character of the sufferings of Christ. Before, however, I proceed immediately to the subject, I think it necessary to offer a few preliminary remarks.

The atonement of Christ was a strictly equitable transaction. But, as I have just intimated, there are parts of the divine government which we find difficult to reconcile with the acknowledged perfections of the Deity. I have no disposition, however, to avail myself of this fact in order to get rid of any of the supposed objections to the doctrine now under consideration. We believe it to be the most grand and illustrious judicial proceeding that ever took place in the universe. We esteem it the most convincing and eminent demonstration of the righteousness of God. It might naturally be expected, therefore, that such revelations respecting it would be afforded to man as might enable him to discern its perfect righteousness, as well as its distinguished mercy. This, I believe, is indeed the fact, as I hope to be enabled to show. I will not avail myself of the mysteries of divine justice, but employ in the argument those views on the subject of justice which are commonly admitted among men. And even with this concession, I trust I shall satisfy you that the vicarious suffering of Christ was strictly equitable; that it possesses that abounding meritoriousness which renders it available to the judicial exigencies of man; and that Christ was the only being in the universe who was capable of thus at once demonstrating the divine rectitude, and relieving us in our miserable condition.

In order to render a vicarious sacrifice just and available, the following things are necessary:—

1. That there shall be no obligation on the sufferer.
2. That he shall himself be the subject of reward.
3. That the ends of justice shall be more fully answered by the suffering of the substitute than by that of the actual offender.
4. That the offended party shall be satisfied with the substitute, and shall afford sufficient evidence of his admission of it.
5. That the offender shall accept the suffering of the substitute upon such terms as he shall be pleased to propose.

I call this an argument upon the harmony of the atonement; and I employ the term in two senses: first, in reference to the attributes of God; and, secondly, in the mutual relation of its several parts, by which it assumes a proper systematized character. Now I think it is evident that if it can be proved that our views of the doctrine of the atonement are harmonious in themselves, and consistent with the divine character, there will be everything but demonstration of their truth. At all events they will be rendered so probable as to allow of little further dispute. And if beyond this they can be shown to harmonize with the general tenor of Scripture, while every other theory is at utter variance with it, the proof will be complete. Both I hope to be able to do; and nothing will afford me greater satisfaction than to find that this train of argument assists you to dismiss your doubts upon the subject, and to return with renewed and vigorous faith to those enjoyments which this doctrine alone can supply.

Letter IX.

My dear Friend,

The first requisite for a vicarious sacrifice is the freedom of the sufferer from obligation. Obligation, as applied to a law, is of two kinds. The one refers to its requirements, and may be described as moral: the other results from its sanctions, and may be distinguished as judicial. In the case of the divine law, the first is that which binds all creatures to obedience; and the second, that whereby all sinners are compelled to submit to its penalties. The latter excludes the notion of meritoriousness entirely; and the former also, except so far as the individual is concerned whose obedience it secures. Now it is essential to vicarious suffering which shall be beneficial to others, that it should possess an amplitude of merit totally inconsistent with all such obligation. For if it be the duty of any being to suffer, he alone can be benefited by his suffering; while, if his sins have rendered punishment necessary, there is no legal advantage to be derived from it, either to himself or any other.

Now all creatures are bound, by their relation to the

Creator, to do and to endure everything which shall conduce to his glory; or, in other words, everything that consists with his will. No virtuous act can in them be supererogatory; for such is the amplitude of their obligation, that they can never transcend its requisitions. It is essential to their nature, and commensurate to all its powers and resources. It matters not that their obedience is voluntary; that it results from the most ardent desire to please God; or that it is accompanied by the most satisfactory evidences of their devotion to his will. When they have done everything of which the most exalted created power is capable; when they have taxed their energies to the utmost; when they have employed countless ages in the most vigilant purity and the most accurate obedience, they have only fulfilled their obligation thus far; and all that they can challenge from God is the reward due to individual virtue. This is the law of the entire intelligent creation, embracing the first and the lowest, the most perfect and the most mean.

If God, therefore, has appointed any individual to suffer for the sin of man, his first qualification must be the most perfect and immaculate moral purity, a freedom from every sort of taint or depravity; otherwise, his suffering is for himself exclusively, and even to himself can be of no judicial advantage. He must also be independent of all the obligation under which every creature is laid; else the benefit of his suffering will be confined to himself. It is not enough to say that his submission to suffering is voluntary; because that is required from every creature in all the acts which God appoints. An act may be voluntary, and yet consist with obligation; which, as I have just shown, excludes all redundant meritoriousness.

Now we maintain that Christ possesses both these qualifications; that he was not only free from stain, but more than a creature; that he was really and essentially God; that his sufferings were not only voluntary, but perfectly independent of all obligation; that while their voluntary character relieves the atonement from the suspicion of injustice, the absolute spontaneity of it endows it with the most abundant and satisfactory meritoriousness. Let us look at each of these particulars more minutely.

The first qualification of Christ was his perfect purity. This is so important a feature of his character, and so essential to the efficacy of the atonement, that it was in various ways held up to the contemplation of the faithful for many ages before his actual advent. In the types of the Mosaic law there was the utmost scrupulosity required to ascertain that all the victims were free from blemish, and the slightest imperfection was sufficient to vitiate the sacrifice. That this observance was designed to indicate the purity of Christ, St. Peter's allusion to the subject is sufficient to assure us: "Ye were not redeemed," says the Apostle, "with corruptible things, but with the precious blood of Christ, as of a lamb without blemish and without spot, who verily was foreordained before the foundation of the world." (1 Pet. i. 18-20.) The testimony of the Prophets is also abundant to the purity of Christ; and thus was the expectation of men particularly excited to this feature of his character.

It was, however, necessary that Christ should possess a truly human and mortal nature, and that, principally, that he might be made subject to a penal death. Human nature is polluted; and hence it was essential to his work that he should assume it in some such peculiar method as would at once secure its real and essential humanity, and provide for its freedom from its hereditary taint. This was effected by his conception in a virgin's womb, through the immediate agency of the Holy Spirit. I am not now about to philosophize upon this mysterious subject. It will be early enough for us to do that when we comprehend the process of ordinary generation. Of the fact we have every assurance which the testimony of God can afford; and more than this it is impious to require. This was, indeed, so remarkable a feature in Christ's character, as to be the subject of distinct prophecy. It was conveyed in the first promise; for whereas ordinary posterity is attributed to the father, as the children of the Patriarchs are called "the seed of Abraham" and "the seed of Jacob," He is emphatically designated as "the seed of the woman." The testimony of Isaiah is still more unequivocal: "A virgin shall conceive and bear a son, and shall call his name Emmanuel,"—a prophecy which, St. Matthew expressly states, was fulfilled in the conception and birth of Christ.

Beyond this, it seems to have been highly expedient, if not really necessary, that the purity of Christ's nature should be evidenced by his dwelling among men, and exhibiting to them a perfect example; that he should be tested by the various inducements and temptations which are common to humanity; that thus the most convincing assurance of his qualifications for his work might be afforded to us. Accordingly, he was tempted in all points like as we, yet without sin. He has left us an example, that we should tread in his steps. He was holy, harmless, undefiled, and separate from sinners; and, to confirm our confidence, God testified from heaven, "This is my beloved Son, in whom I am well pleased."

Such were some of the qualifications of Christ for his stupendous work. The justice of God could make no exception to such a victim. Infernal spirits acknowledged him as "the *Holy* One of God;" and men, scarcely less malignant, gnashed their teeth, and were silent. Angels ministered unto him; and, for the first time, heaven heard arise from earth those appropriate words of spotless triumph, "Father, I have glorified thee on the earth: I have finished the work which thou gavest me to do." (John xvii. 4.)

I am not concerned, in this place, to go at large into the evidence of the doctrine of Christ's proper Deity, since that cannot be gainsaid except by rejecting those principles of Scripture interpretation which I have already proved to be fixed and unalterable. Thus, in the first verse of St. John's Gospel, we are told that "the Word was God;" and this declaration, Bishop Middleton has shown, is incapable of any other rendering. The same Evangelist proceeds to say, that "all things were made by him," and that "without him was not anything made which was made:" or, if we admit the Socinian translation of this passage, we have still the same doctrine, according to the Socinians themselves, in the first chapter of the Epistle to the Colossians. The "Improved Version" thus translates the 16th and following verses of that chapter: "By him all things were created that are in heaven, and that are on earth, visible and invisible, whether they be thrones, or dominions, or principalities, or powers: all these* things were created by him and for him, and he is before all things, and by him these* things subsist." One would hardly suppose it possible that any attempt would be made to evade the force of such a passage; yet such there has been. We are not to suppose that Christ made the heavens and the earth, we are told, but only the things in them; that is, he was the Creator of the sun, the planets, and the stars, the atmosphere, the light, all spiritual intelligences, the human race, and all animal and vegetable existences, but not of the heavens or the earth. I confess myself unable to comprehend the force of this exception. If, however, it have any meaning, (which with my present views, I most seriously doubt,) it is wholly nullified by

---

*The word "these" is not in the original, and is inserted without any sort of acknowledgment by the editors of the Improved Version. They have not even taken the precaution to put it in Italics. The original is simply τα παντα.

the following part of the passage, — "all things were created by him and for him," τα παντα, the most ample and comprehensive term which could have been employed. Christ was therefore the Creator of all things; and he that created all things is God. (Heb. iii. 4.) I think I need not multiply proof on this subject.

If, therefore, Christ be really God, he must be perfectly independent of all extrinsic obligation, and whatever he does must be done spontaneously. The spring of all his purposes and acts must be in himself, not as excluding the other persons of the Trinity, but as conjoined with them in simultaneous harmony. The Deity must impel itself independently of everything external. This is essential to the divine nature and perfections; and though we are compelled and allowed to employ terms which represent God as affected and determined in his conduct by that which is outward, yet, in truth, there is no divine act which does not originate in the divine mind. This explains what I mean by spontaneity, as distinguished from voluntariness. The work of the atonement must therefore have resulted from the spontaneous benevolence of the Deity; and all that Christ did in reference to it, till the moment he assumed our nature, must have partaken of the same character. This view is confirmed by various passages of Scripture. Hence the love of Christ is represented as "passing knowledge;" (Eph. iii. 19;) a phrase not applicable to it, except upon the admission of the foregoing view. For it may be safely affirmed, that there is no submission to the will of God so ample as to be beyond comprehension. We may not fully understand the capacity of all intelligences; but so far as we do understand it, we are not at any loss to conceive of their being perfectly submitted to the divine will. There is no proper sense of the term, therefore, in which the love of a creature passeth knowledge, because we know every sort of love of which a creature is capable. But the love of Christ is incomprehensible, not merely because Christ, as God, is infinite, but because its origination was independent of every law. We are incapable of conceiving of a love which it is not our duty to cherish; but the love of Christ was, in the first place, completely abstracted from every sort of obligation.

I think we may safely say, that the absolute spontaneity of the work of the atonement gives it its peculiar virtue. Our notions of virtue are generally determined by its voluntariness. The highest virtue of the creature is a perfect submission to the will of God. Yet even in this we are able to institute certain distinctions; for where there is much to invite to duty, and little to deter from it, we assign a lower degree of merit than where the strength of principle is tested by the absence of many external inducements, and the opposition of many repelling circumstances. Of course, the most exalted virtue of which we can conceive is that of the atonement, — a work to which there was no consciousness of obligation, and which originated in the independent and spontaneous love of Christ, — the scheme of which was matured, abstracted from all the lower considerations of inducement or opposition. To this there appears some allusion where Christ attributes the special love of the Father to the laying down of his life by an absolutely spontaneous act: "Therefore doth my Father love me, because I lay down my life, that I may take it again. No man taketh it from me, but I lay it down of myself." (John x, 17, 18.)

And even after Christ had assumed the form of a servant and become subject to the laws of human nature, we find that the accomplishment of his work was a passion with him. It was his meat and drink; his zeal for it was all-absorbing; and he represents himself as in pain till he should have fulfilled the designs of his love. "I have," says he, "a baptism to be baptized with, and how am I straitened till it be accomplished." Amidst inconceivable opposition, and crowds of unspeakable horrors, this grand principle upheld him, till the work of his expiation was complete, and he dismissed his spirit.

These views will enable you to perceive, that the meritoriousness of the work of the atonement was inconceivable and infinite. It was an act of virtue of which every other being in the universe was, by his nature, incapable: and faint and weak as are our views upon it, they still afford us a glimpse of the meaning of the emphatic declaration, "God is love!" Will you forgive me if I add a glowing passage from a poet whose works merit more attention than is commonly accorded to them?

"O blessed well of Love! O flower of Grace!
O glorious Morning Starre! O Lampe of Light!
Most lively image of thy Father's face,
   Eternal King of Glorie, Lord of might,
   Meeke Lambe of God, before all worlds behight,
How can we thee requite for all this good?
Or what can prize that thy most precious blood!"

Suffer me then, my dear friend, to beg your most serious consideration of the topics suggested in this letter, and to ask, "Whose image and superscription is this?" Is it possible that such a theory should have originated in the fancy of man? Is it credible that fallible man should by chance have stumbled upon such a concatenation of doctrines? Each of the doctrines to which we have now alluded (the Deity, immaculate conception, and atonement of Christ) is obviously beyond the range of human speculation, and by the exertion of mere human faculty would never have been dreamed of. You see how they harmonize, how each is fitted into the other, and how the admission of one naturally, if not necessarily, leads to that of the others; and again I ask, is it possible that the whole is error, a mere dream of enthusiasm, by which the majority of the church have been deluded for centuries? Is it the province of error to introduce such a system of unexceptionable harmony? Has there ever been such another instance in the history of the human mind? Where there is error, especially error in principle, there will be distortion and obliquity. No system of falsehood is in concord with itself; and it may be added, that no plausible system of error ever existed without the mixture of truth. But here all is fallacious, if one doctrine be so. There is no truth, if there be any mistake. You must take all, or none. Your admission or rejection must be entire.

I venture on these arks here, because I have already introduced the most purely supernatural doctrines with which that of the atonement is associated, and because I think that they are remarkable for the confirmation which they mutually supply. So much so, in fact, that I am at a loss to understand how their united force can be evaded. But I wish you also to observe, that the harmony of the other parts of the atonement is not less than that which has now been stated; and I have therefore hinted at the mode of its application, that you may the more fully avail yourself of the suggestions of my subsequent letters.

Letter X.

My dear Friend,

It will at once occur to you, that the allegation of injustice against the vicarious suffering of Christ is exceedingly idle, so long as our views are confined to his divinity, and the consequent absolute spontaneity of his atonement. But the subject assumes a different aspect when we come to the contemplation of his humanity, and his relation to the laws of man's nature and dispensation. In this view, we discern the necessity of a reward being affixed to his work, in order to the preservation of the equity of the transaction: and this is the second requisite to a just and available substitution of the innocent for the guilty. It is, I think, most clearly admitted in the Scriptures, that no individual is the subject of virtuous suffering, the benefit of which is not confined to himself, without being either in this world or hereafter the recipient of direct reward. Although it is scarcely possible for a pious mind to be visited by calamity, no matter from what quarter, or for what end, without personal improvement and general moral advantage. However great the benefits, therefore, which are thus extended to others, the profit of the individual sufferer is usually so considerable as to preclude the abstract necessity of reward on account of his endurance. But such is the benevolent constitution of the divine government, that no measure of virtue is permitted to go unrewarded. Nor does any personal advantage resulting immediately from its exercise, appear to be adverted to in the distribution of a divine reward. In harmony, therefore, with the general principles of God's administration, it was necessary that Christ should be the subject of a reward.

Now, as the virtue of Christ was transcendent and unparalleled, and as the direct personal advantage resulting from it (if, indeed, such an advantage existed at all) was, comparatively, exceedingly insignificant, it seems only fitting that his reward should be of the most signal and eminent order; and since his sufferings were endured by the special appointment of God, and were manifested to mankind at large, it also appears proper that his reward should immediately from God himself, and should be sufficiently illustrious to awake the attention and admiration of all men. Thus far we might conjecture, independently of any direct testimony of the Scriptures.

There is also another view of the subject which ought not to be forgotten. When Christ assumed human nature, he came under the influence of the ordinary laws by which it is regulated. One of the most obvious of these is the necessity of the expectation of reward, in order to the maintenance of a course of piety, and especially to a holy submission to those ills which befall us by divine permission or appointment. The hope of reward, it is to be remarked, does not exclusively belong to the present degenerate condition of man, since, in his original state of innocence, our great progenitor was to be deterred from sin by the threatening of punishment. And if he were capable of being affected by the more servile motive of fear, as it is clear, from the fact, that he was, much more was he the subject of the nobler motive of hope. It follows, that man, in his best state, was made to be impelled by the desire of advantage; and this is, therefore, one of the essential principles of humanity. When Christ became man, he, of course, came under the influence of this law; and as the purest minds are always most fully swayed by the hope of the honours which attend upon devotion to God, there is every reason to believe that on the mind of Christ the perception of those blessings which awaited his successful labours and sufferings, made an unusually deep impression. This was the more necessary, as his duties were of so oppressive a nature. And this is the representation given us by the author of the Epistle to the Hebrews: "For the joy that was set before him," says this writer, "he endured the cross and despised the shame." This testimony, it is easy to discern, is worded so as to convey the notion not merely that Christ submitted to unavoidable evil without complaint, but his mind was so raised by the contemplation of his reward as to be insensible to the common impressions of infamy, which, under other circumstances, might have given a less noble and determined tone to his general behaviour.

In ordinary cases, reward neutralises merit; that is to say, where a being is rewarded to the full proportion of his virtue, it is not to be expected that the meritoriousness of his conduct can be applied to the benefit of any other person. There is in such a case, if I may so express it, no redundancy of meritoriousness. But the reward given to Christ is accorded to his humanity. His deity cannot be the subject of accession of glory and happiness, and the absolute spontaneity of his vicarious work is, therefore, unaffected in its infinite meritoriousness by any reward, however exalted.

Nor is this all: Christ, by his suffering, has rendered

unnecessary the perpetuation of the former legal covenant under which Adam was placed. It may, therefore, be abrogated without at all derogating from the dignity of the law. And the ancient covenant, in which Adam was the representative of the human race, being thus laid aside, there is room and necessity for a new covenant. The reward which Christ claims is, that such a covenant shall be established, in which he shall be the federal head of mankind. While, therefore, he secures to himself the highest honour, it is only that he may thus place himself at the head of the mediatorial kingdom, and every gem of his diadem is made to beam peace and pardon upon our lapsed and miserable race.

Whether, therefore, we contemplate him as God or as man, or, more properly, as uniting in himself both the one and the other, we perceive the infinite fitness of the doctrine of his vicarious work. If we regard him as God, we see infinite dignity in his person, stamping all that he does with the highest value, combined with benevolence, absolutely independent and spontaneous, giving the highest legal meritoriousness to whatever sufferings his humanity might undergo. If we consider him as man, we perceive him admitted to the enjoyment of the highest rewards and honour; while, if we contemplate his mixed character, we behold him seated on a throne of grace, honoured, indeed, according to the fitness of his claims, but employing the very blessings which belong to him personally for the restoration and the happiness of his creatures,—a Prince and a Saviour.

From this brief epitome of the subject, I turn your attention to the direct testimony of Scripture in its confirmation. I may first notice some of those passages which speak of the glory of Christ in general, and then refer you to some statements of a more particular kind. When the author of the Epistle to the Hebrews draws a contrast between the eminence of Christ and that of angels, he represents God as putting the highest honour on him, in consequence of his exalted rectitude and purity; and for this purpose quotes Psalm xlv. 7: "Thou hast loved righteousness and hated iniquity; therefore God, thy God, hath anointed thee with the oil of gladness above thy fellows." (Heb. i. 9.) Christ himself attributes the honour put upon him by the Father to his having assumed our nature: "As the Father hath life in himself, so hath he given to the Son to have life in himself, and hath given him authority to execute judgment also, because he is the Son of man." (John v. 26, 27.) In the same chapter he also states the specific purpose for which this authority was thus committed to him: "The Father judgeth no man, but hath committed all judgment unto the Son, that all men should honour the Son even as they honour the Father;" and so fully is the glory of God concerned in this arrangement, that the Father is represented as identified in all the devotion paid to the Son: "He that honoureth not the Son, honoureth not the Father which hath sent him;" (verses 22, 23;) a sentiment which, I need hardly add, is of frequent occurrence in the New Testament.

Again: in Psalm lxxii. the universal dominion of Christ is attributed to the eminence and tenderness of his benevolence: "All Kings shall fall down before him; all nations shall serve him: for he shall deliver the needy when he crieth; the poor also, and him that hath no helper. He shall spare the poor and needy." (Verse 11, *et seq.*) By the Prophet Isaiah, the successful consummation of his expiatory work is represented as the cause of his exaltation: "Behold, my servant shall deal prudently, he shall be exalted and extolled, and be very high. As many were astonished at thee [on account of the extremity of thy suffering); his visage was so marred more than any man, and his form more than the sons of men: so shall he sprinkle* many nations; [extending the purifying influence of his blood to the ends of the earth;] the Kings shall shut their mouths at him: [none offering the slightest opposition to claims of him whose sufferings filled them with astonishment:] for that which had not been told them shall they see; and that which they had not heard shall they consider." [The strange history of the suffering of Christ shall be brought before the contemplation of Gentile Sovereigns, and the result shall be, the admission of his right.] (Isaiah lii. 13-15.) And again, after the Prophet has spoken of the pleasure of the Lord prospering in the hand of Christ, it is added,—

> "Therefore will I distribute to him the many for his portion,
> And the mighty people shall he share for his spoil,
> BECAUSE he poured out his soul unto death,
> And was numbered with the transgressors,
> And he bare the sin of many,
> And made intercession for the transgressors."
> LOWTH'S Isaiah. (liii. 12.)

The honour bestowed upon him, Christ himself represents as the result of the glory which the consummation of his work reflected on the Father. Upon Judas's retirement from the last supper to complete his traitorous design, He exclaims, "Now is the Son of man glorified, and God is glorified in him. If God be glorified in him, God shall also glorify him in himself, and shall straightway glorify him." (John xiii. 31, 32.)

---

*Or, perhaps, causing the ministry of the word to fall upon many nations, as some Rabbinical critics explain it. Others, in compliance with the version of the Seventy, read it,

> "So, many nations shall look on him with admiration:
> Kings shall stop their mouths," &c.
> DR. JEBB. See LOWTH, in loc.

In which case the sense appears to be, that astonishment at the sufferings of Christ shall be followed by universal admiration and admission of his claims.

The testimony of the sacred writers as to Christ's assumption of the mediatorial throne, and consequent triumphs, being the reward of his expiatory work, is exceedingly explicit. In some of the following passages you will find it distinctly stated, in others certainly involved: "And you, being dead in your sins, hath he quickened, blotting out the handwriting of ordinances that was against us, nailing it to his cross; having spoiled principalities and powers, he made a show of them openly, triumphing over them in it." (Col. ii. 13-15.) In Heb. i. 3, 4, it is said of the Son, that being "the brightness of the Father's glory, and the express image of his person, and upholding all things by the word of his power, having by himself purged our sins, he sat down on the right hand of the Majesty on high; being as much better than angels, as he hath obtained, by right of inheritance, a more excellent title or rank than they." That is, as I understand it, the mediatorial glory of Christ, which he has assumed upon the ground of having purged our sins, is as far above that glory which angels possess through their agency in God's government, as his original rank was superior to theirs. He is the Son, (verse 5,) but they are only servants. (Verse 7.) He has an everlasting and unchangeable government over his people, to whom angels are but ministering spirits. This argument the writer pursues thus: The Gospel dispensation is not subject to angels. (Heb. ii. 5.) But to human nature in the person of Christ all things were to be subjected, although for a little while he was in that nature inferior to angels. The reason why he was thus humbled, was that he might taste death for every man; a work so full of virtue and merit, that, as the Syriac version gives it, "We see Jesus for the suffering of death crowned with glory and honour." The writer then proceeds to argue, that this reward of the endurance of Christ, was in the highest degree fitting. "It became him for whom are all things, and by whom are all things, to bestow, on account of sufferings, the highest honours upon Him, who is the Captain of their salvation, leading many sons to glory." (Stuart's Translation, Heb. ii. 10.) One of the very important functions of the mediatorial kingdom, the developement [sic] of the designs of God's moral government, is expressly ascribed to Christ on the ground of the meritoriousness of his expiatory work, and that by the noblest and most glorious of creatures: "And when he," the Lamb, "had taken the book, the four beasts and four-and-twenty elders fell down before the Lamb, having every one of them harps, and golden vials full of odours, which are the prayers of saints. And they sung a new song, saying, Thou art worthy to take the book, and to open the seals thereof: for thou wast slain, and hast redeemed us to God by thy blood out of every kindred, and tongue, and people, and nation; and hast made us unto our God kings and priests: and we shall reign on the earth. And I beheld, and I heard the voice of many angels round about the throne and the beasts and the elders: and the number of them was ten thousand times ten thousand, and thousands of thousands; saying with a loud voice, Worthy is the Lamb that was slain to receive power, and riches, and wisdom, and strength, and honour, and glory, and blessing. And every creature which is in heaven, and on the earth, and under the earth, and such as are in the sea, and all that are in them, heard I saying, Blessing, and honour, and glory, and power, be unto him that sitteth upon the throne, and unto the Lamb for ever and ever. And the four beasts said, Amen. And the four-and-twenty elders fell down and worshipped him that liveth for ever and ever." (Rev. v. 8-14.) The Apostle Paul, in addressing the Philippians, thus states the glorious and triumphant results of Christ's humiliation and obedience: "Let this mind be in you, which was also in Christ Jesus: who, being in the form of God, thought it not robbery to be equal with God: but made himself of no reputation, and took upon him the form of a servant, and was made in the likeness of men: and being found in fashion as a man, he humbled himself, and became obedient unto death, even the death of the cross. Wherefore God also hath highly exalted him, and given him a name which is above every name: that at the name of JESUS every knee should bow, of things in heaven, and things in earth, and things under the earth; and that every tongue should confess that Jesus Christ is Lord, to the glory of God the Father." (Phil. ii. 5-11.) And that all this glory is that of Christ's mediatorship, and designed for the blessing of man, may be gathered from a multitude of passages: "To him that overcometh will I grant to sit with me in my throne, even as I also overcame, and am set down with my Father in his throne." (Rev. iii. 21.) "Him hath God exalted with his right hand to be a Prince and a Saviour, for to give repentance to Israel, and forgiveness of sins." (Acts v. 31.) "Wherefore he saith, When he ascended up on high, he led captivity captive, and gave gifts unto men. (Now that he ascended, what is it but that he also descended first into the lower parts of the earth? He that descended is the same also that ascended up far above all heavens, that he might fill all things.) And he gave some, Apostles; and some, Prophets; and some, Evangelists; and some, Pastors and Teachers; for the perfecting of the saints, for the work of the ministry, for the edifying of the body of Christ: till we all come in the unity of the faith, and of the knowledge of the Son of God, unto a perfect man, unto the measure of the stature of the fulness of Christ," &c. (Eph iv. 8-13.) And so abundantly are these advantages to be realized, that even the benevolence of Christ himself is to be satisfied.

> "Of the travail of his soul he shall see [the fruit,] and be satisfied:
> By the knowledge of him shall my righteous servant justify many;

For the punishment of their iniquities he shall bear."
LOWTH'S *Isaiah*. (liii. 11.)

From these and similar scriptures, I hope it will be evident to you that all the blessings which we receive under the Gospel dispensation, partake of the nature of rewards to Christ himself. That his assumption of his mediatorial dignity was necessary to their communication, and especially to the communication of the influences of the Holy Spirit, is plain from several express statements of our Lord himself, as well as of the Evangelists. Turn to John vii. 37-39, and you will find that the influences of the Spirit are there made to depend upon the glorification of Christ: "In the last day, that great day of the feast, Jesus stood and cried, saying, If any man thirst, let him come unto me, and drink. He that believeth on me, as the Scripture hath said, out of his belly shall flow rivers of living water. (But this spake he of the Spirit, which they that believe on him should receive: for the Holy Ghost was not yet given; because that Jesus was not yet glorified.)" It is not to be doubted, that the blessings described in this passage were those sanctifying illapses of that blessed agent, which are common to Christians. In John xvi. 7-15, Christ himself is still more explicit: "Nevertheless I tell you the truth: It is expedient for you that I go away: for if I go not away, the Comforter will not come unto you; but if I depart, I will send him unto you. And when he is come, he will reprove the world of sin, and of righteousness, and of judgment: of sin, because they believe not on me: of righteousness, because I go my Father, and ye see me no more: of judgment, because the prince of this world is judged. I have yet many things to say unto you, but ye cannot bear them now. Howbeit when he, the Spirit of truth, is come, he will guide you into all truth: for he shall not speak of himself; but whatsoever he shall hear, that shall he speak: and he will show you things to come. He shall glorify me: for he shall receive of mine, and shall show it unto you. All things that the Father hath are mine: therefore said I, that he shall take of mine, and show it unto you." He here declares that the effusion of the Spirit, in his convincing influences, was the direct and essential result of his returning to the Father; and although there is occasionally in the communications of Christ to his disciples a reference to the extraordinary operations of the Spirit, yet this is by no means the most prominent view which these statements supply. "And I will pray the Father, and he shall give you another Comforter, that he may abide with you for ever; even the Spirit of truth; whom the world cannot receive, because it seeth him not, neither knoweth him; but ye know him, for he dwelleth with you, and shall be in you." "But the Comforter, which is the Holy Ghost, whom the Father will send in my name, he shall teach you all things, and bring all things to your remembrance, whatsoever I have said unto you." (John xiv. 16, 26.) "But when the Comforter is come, whom I will send unto you from the Father, even the Spirit of truth, which proceedeth from the Father, he shall testify of me." (John xv. 26.)

I know not whether it be necessary for me to add, that all evangelical blessings are dispensed to us through the covenant, in which Christ is the representative of the human race, and in which he sustains to us a similar relation to that of Adam in the original covenant. "Nevertheless death reigned from Adam to Moses, even over them that had not sinned after the similitude of Adam's transgression, who is the figure of him that was to come. But not as the offence, so also is the free gift. For if through the offence of one many be dead, much more the grace of God, and the gift by grace, which is by one man, Jesus Christ, hath abounded unto many. And not as it was by one that sinned, so is the gift: for the judgment was by one to condemnation, but the free gift is of many offences unto justification. For if by one man's offence death reigned by one; much more they which receive abundance of grace and of the gift of righteousness shall reign in life by one, Jesus Christ. Therefore as by the offence of one judgment came upon all men to condemnation; even so by the righteousness of one the free gift came upon all men unto justification of life. For as by one man's disobedience many were made sinners, so by the obedience of one shall many be made righteous. Moreover the law entered, that the offence might abound. But where sin abounded, grace did much more abound: that as sin hath reigned unto death, even so might grace reign through righteousness unto eternal life by Jesus Christ our Lord." (Rom. v. 14-21.) "Christ hath redeemed us from the curse of the law, being made a curse for us: for it is written, Cursed is every one that hangeth on a tree: that the blessing of Abraham might come on the Gentiles through Jesus Christ; that we might receive the promise of the Spirit through faith." "But the Scripture hath concluded all under sin, that the promise by faith of Jesus Christ might be given to them that believe. But before faith came, we were kept under the law, shut up unto the faith which should afterwards be revealed. Wherefore the law was our schoolmaster to bring us unto Christ, that we might be justified by faith. But after that faith is come, we are no longer under a schoolmaster. For ye are all the children of God by faith in Christ Jesus." (Gal. iii. 13, 14, 22-26.) "If therefore perfection were by the Levitical priesthood, (for under it the people received the law,) what further need was there that another Priest should rise after the order of Melchisedec, and not be called after the order of Aaron?" "For it is evident that our Lord sprang out of Juda; of which tribe Moses spake nothing concerning priesthood. And it is yet far more evident: for that after the similitude of Melchisedec there ariseth another Priest, who is made, not after the law of a carnal commandment, but after the power of an endless life." "And inasmuch as not without an oath he was made Priest: by so much was Jesus made a surety of a better testament. And they truly were many Priests, because they were not suffered to continue by reason of death: but this man, because he continueth ever, hath an unchangeable priesthood. Wherefore he is able also to save them to the uttermost that come unto God by him, seeing he ever liveth to make intercession for them." (Heb. vii. 11, 14-16, 20, 22-25.) "But now hath he obtained a more excellent ministry, by how much also he is the mediator of a better covenant, which was established upon better promises. For if that first covenant had been faultless, then should no place have been sought for the second. For finding fault with them, he saith, Behold, the days come, saith the Lord, when I will make a new covenant with the house of Israel and with the house of Judah: not according to the covenant that I made with their fathers in the day when I took them by the hand to lead them out of the land of Egypt; because they continued not in my covenant, and I regarded them not, saith the Lord. For this is the covenant that I will make with the house of Israel after those days, saith the Lord; I will put my laws into their mind, and write them in their hearts: and I will be to them a God, and they shall be to me a people: and they shall not teach every man his brother, saying, Know the Lord: for all shall know me, from the least to the greatest. For I will be merciful to their unrighteousness, and their sins and their iniquities will I remember no more." (Heb. viii. 6-12.) "And for this cause he is the Mediator of the new testament, that by means of death, for the redemption of the transgressions that were under the first testament, they which are called might receive the promise of eternal inheritance." (Heb. ix. 15.) "Then said he, Lo, I come to do thy will, O God. He taketh away the first, that he may establish the second. By the which will we are sanctified through the offering of the body of Jesus Christ once for all. And every Priest standeth daily ministering and offering oftentimes the same sacrifices, which can never take away sins: but this man, after he had offered one sacrifice for sins, for ever sat down on the right hand of God; from henceforth expecting till his enemies be made his footstool. For by one offering he hath perfected for ever them that are sanctified." "Having therefore, brethren, boldness to enter into the holiest by the blood of Jesus, by a new and living way, which he hath consecrated for us, through the veil, that is to say, his flesh; and having an High-Priest over the house of God; let us draw near with a true heart in full assurance of faith, having our hearts sprinkled from an evil conscience, and our bodies washed with pure water." (Heb. x. 9-14, 19-22.) "For since by man came death, by man came also the resurrection of the dead. For as in Adam all die, even so in Christ shall all be made alive." (1 Cor. xv. 21, 22.)

An argument in favour of the foregoing views of no inconsiderable weight, may, I think, be deduced from the analogy between them, and the generally received opinions upon the subject of the divine government in general. The latter, I suppose, is universally admitted to be eminently benevolent in its principles. The attributes and glory of God, if I may so speak, are made subservient to the happiness of his creatures. No system of religion, except some forms of Paganism, represents the Deity as seated in solitary and silent grandeur, abstracted from the concerns of creation, shedding no genial influences upon the beings whom he has made, and dwelling in a selfish recklessness as to whether they are happy or wretched. No; thus far at least there is extensive unanimity. We attribute to our Creator a paternal interest in his creatures; we believe that he employs his power and his wisdom, and fills the universe with a spirit of benign joy. We believe, that he is intensely concerned to render his intelligent creation the sharers of his purity and happiness; and we readily reject any doctrine which tends to limit these exhibitions of divine benevolence.

Such is the character of the natural government of God. But, if the Bible be credible, there is nothing more true than that the evangelical scheme is one of transcendent benevolence; and hence, while the sacred writers dwell occasionally upon the revelations of the divine goodness in his ordinary administration, they are perpetually bringing before us the arrangements of the Gospel, as the peculiar evidences of his benignity. But abandon the views which we have just stated, and I confess I am quite at a loss to perceive the consistency of these representations. Say that the glory of Christ is the mere reward of individual virtue, and that the benefits which result from it are only casual and accidental,—just as the perfume from the sanctuary might reach the senses of the worshippers in the outer court,—and it is trifling with the subject to exalt this as an arrangement of transcendent benevolence. Suppose that Christ is rewarded in the full proportion of his merit, but that his reward affects his people no farther than that of any glorified saint, and it is absurd to compare his glory with that of the liberality of the God of providence. To justify the scriptural representations of the transcendent benignity of Christ in his glory, it is absolutely necessary that it should more fully redound to the advantage of man, than any of the exhibitions of goodness in the ordinary administration of human affairs; and this can only be done upon the admission, that the reward of Christ consists in his mediatorial elevation, and the establishment of his mediatorial covenant. With this view, we at once discern that the glory of Christ not only harmonizes with that displayed in the providential conduct of the universe, but infinitely exceeds it in the blessings to be ensured by it. No other doctrine can be otherwise than inconsistent with the plain declarations of the Bible; and by the only admissible laws of interpretation, therefore, no other doctrine can be otherwise than false.

But I will not further anticipate topics, to which I shall, in a future letter, have occasion more amply to refer.

Letter XI.

MY DEAR FRIEND,

IN THE EPISTLE TO the Romans, the following remarkable passage occurs:— "But now the righteousness of God without the law is manifested, being witnessed by the law and the Prophets; even the righteousness of God which is by faith of Jesus Christ unto all and upon all them that believe: for there is no difference: for all have sinned, and come short of the glory of God; being justified freely by his grace through the redemption that is in Christ Jesus: whom God hath set forth to be a propitiation through faith in his blood, to declare his righteousness for the remission of sins that are past, through the forbearance of God; to declare I say at this time his righteousness: that he might be just, and the justifier of him which believeth in Jesus." (Rom. iii. 21-26.) This passage immediately follows a declaration of the utter inability of the law to justify any human being; and in it we find the Apostle asserting that without the intervention of the law, God might be just, even while he justified a sinner. This is represented as the effect of Christ's propitiation;

and the especial ground of the value of this propitiation as here stated is, that it was a display of God's righteousness. And this brings us immediately to the third requisite for a just and available vicarious sacrifice; namely, that the suffering of a substitute shall answer the ends of justice more fully than that of the actual offender. I say "more fully," because a perfectly righteous governor can have no inducement to deviate from the ordinary process of retribution, except upon this admission. In the case before us, a legal covenant cannot be supposed to be justly abrogated, except to give place to a covenant more fully illustrative of the divine righteousness. Justice, and not mercy, is the essential attribute of every good government; and it is the perfect satisfaction of justice alone that can afford room for the exercise of benevolence. It will, therefore, be my object to show, that the substitution of the innocent for the guilty, in the case of the death of Christ, was a more perfect accomplishment of the designs of justice, than the actual punishment of the whole human race.

Before, however, I go immediately to the consideration of the subject, it may be proper to remind you, that we have reason to believe that God and man are not the only beings interested in this very important question. God, it is true, is the moral Governor of the world, but he is equally the Sovereign of the universe; and throughout the whole creation, there is not one pure intelligence who is not more or less concerned for the divine honour and rectitude. It is likely, that of the majority of these we are entirely ignorant, and although there is great probability that the universe is extensively peopled with them, yet their existence is only matter of speculation and conjecture. Of certain orders, however, of glorious and unspotted intellects, the Bible makes certain statements, which, though neither numerous nor explicit, are yet sufficient to assure us of their lively interest in the affairs of mortals. Before these august spirits, God condescends in a peculiar manner to unveil the perfections of his nature, and the principles of his government; and thus is the heavenly world filled with the songs of perpetual joy, and the glow of immortal light and praise. The sufferings of Christ, and the glory that succeeded, are things into which angels desire to look. The constitution of the church is a volume in which they learn the manifold wisdom of God. They worship before the mediatorial throne, and in the new Jerusalem "an innumerable company of angels" are mingled with "the general assembly, and church of the first-born." And yet it is not difficult to prove that, even to their perceptions, the equity of divine government is more fully displayed in the vicarious suffering of Christ, than it would have been by the perdition of the whole of Adam's posterity.

The ends of justice are twofold. The first is a display of the evil of sin, and the excellency of obedience, with a proportionate resentment against the one, and approbation of the other. The second is the encouragement of virtue and the prevention of crime. Practically, these are inseparably connected; but it is necessary to our argument that each should be considered, since the first immediately respects the honour of the Lawgiver, and the second the advantage of those whom he governs; and so far they are distinct views.

It will not be questioned that it is essential to the divine government, that it should in itself be perfectly pure and equitable. I suppose it will also be admitted, that its real character ought to be displayed to all the intelligences under its control, since, as all creatures were made to glorify God, this object cannot be accomplished except by impressions of the perfections of his nature, as made known in his works. If I may so speak, therefore, God owes it to himself to reveal thus far the principles of his conduct to those who are bound to honour him, as, in the absence of such revelations, their devotion cannot be certainly secured. It will be at once perceived that God thus deals with his human family, and the various forms which our submission to him is capable of assuming, are required from us in the Scriptures, upon the ground of certain apposite communications which have been made to us.

There is no impression of the divine character more important than that of his holiness; for the holiness of God is not to be regarded as a distinct attribute like his mercy or his power, but as a quality which pervades his nature, and distinguishes all his attributes and dispensations. Hence his dwelling, his throne, his attendants, his service, and his sacrifices are all distinguished in the Scriptures by their sanctity. But as our notions of abstract purity are faint and indistinct, it is necessary that we should be instructed as to his implacable resentment against sin in every shape. Since also we are not capable of forming any impressive conception of the malignancy of vice apart from sensible illustrations, it has pleased God to supply to all ages the most pregnant examples of its ruinous consequences; and thus the Scriptures are interspersed with fearful histories and still more terrible denunciations, while the analogies of God's providential government clearly confirm the doctrines thus conveyed. So distinctly and variously is this subject brought before us, that it is impossible for any contemplative mind not to discern its illustrations and to admit their force.

The original offence was an act which, considered in itself, was very insignificant; but, as it was an act of disobedience to God's law, it involved the most terrible consequences. Some of these were direct inflictions; others were the natural result of sin itself for it is to be recollected that sin is essentially and unchangeably evil, and does not derive its malignancy from any arbitrary constitution of the divine mind. Though a certain part of its mischievous consequences, therefore, were appended to it by the peculiar judgment of God, the rest would have followed, even if he had not immediately interfered. Attempt then to compute the miseries which have, either naturally or by the divine appointment, resulted from the introduction of sin into the world. Go to the receptacles of wretchedness with which it abounds. Contemplate the vast varieties of agony which the virulence of disease, or the inventions of human cruelty, have inflicted. Listen here to the groans of the travailing woman, and there to the wail of Rachel over her children. Pass from the harvest of death in a field of battle, to the land shaded by the wing of the pestilence. Behold the gaunt form of famine stalking through one realm, and the blast of political tyranny withering the brightest and best beauties of another. Select from history but one picture of invasion or of victory; take but the records of one family, or trace the life of one individual, from the cry helpless infancy to the drivelling of idiot age, the groan of dissolution, the darkness, corruption, and sorrow of the grave; and tell me whether the most vivid imagination of man is not utterly defeated, in an attempt to estimate the melancholy amount of grief which a single spirit may undergo in consequence of sin.

But God has not left us to this detail. In several instances he has come forth from the cloud that surrounds his throne, with the awful insignia of his wrath, to give to all the succeeding ages the terrible impression of his extreme abhorrence of human sin. Need I remind you of the deluge, the destruction of Sodom and the cities of the plain, the overthrow of Jerusalem, and the desolation and dispersion of the Jews? While these facts stand on record, no doubt can be entertained of the extreme and inflexible holiness of the divine character; and for this end, therefore, they are presented to our eyes.

But the punishment which God might have inflicted upon mankind without any impeachment of his equity would have been, beyond all other judgments, the most appalling. He might—who denies his right?—he might have doomed the whole human race to the torments of the second death. He might have blotted the guilty earth out of his universe, or have peopled it with a race of beings more pure and more faithful than man. Nor do I understand how some such signal and eminent exhibition of his severity could have been avoided, had there been no other mode of demonstrating his righteousness. If sin could not have been pardoned by the simple prerogative of God, which would have been no evidence of the divine purity at all, but rather of his connivance at evil, it follows, that every individual sinner must have been punished. This, man's relation to God, and his pure universe, seemed to render unavoidable; and if all have sinned, and every mouth is stopped, there would have been no salvation for any of the human race.

Yet, conclusive as would have been such an evidence of the divine purity, I think there is no difficulty in proving, that the vicarious suffering of Christ was far more impressive, and far more illustrative of God's glory. It was so in respect to the number of intelligent beings who were instructed by it. It is true, that angels would have received a lively impression of God's abhorrence of sin by the destruction of the human race. But it may reasonably be questioned, whether man himself could have shared in this impression. Intense sorrow is absorbing and selfish; it has no capacity for any considerable comprehension beyond its own immediate sphere; and if ever the mind of man, in a state of perdition, could command sufficient calmness to survey the character of God, it would have been so arrayed in severity and terrible indignation as to excite nothing but dreadful emotion. In the vicarious suffering of Christ, the whole human race may behold the most striking exhibition of the divine holiness; but their awe is mixed with admiration, and even love. Wherever the history of the cross has been promulgated, God has been glorified by the spirits of men; and an extensive and benign impression of the divine sanctity has thus been communicated to the human race.

Nor is it the extent of this perception alone which shows the superiority of the vicarious suffering of Christ, but still more fully its depth and vividness. It can hardly be supposed that those spirits who witnessed the lapse and doom of apostate angels could have been very deeply affected by the destruction of a race so far inferior. But the infinite dignity of the person of Christ conferred upon his sufferings not only a legal, but an inconceivable, moral value. It might have been readily conceived, that guilty creatures, however exalted, could not escape the judgment of God; but that He who created all things should ally himself to fallen humanity; and that even the union of the Godhead in his person should not have enabled him to save mankind, without undergoing the penalty of sin, was indeed a most startling representation of its tremendous malignancy, and of the irrevocable determination of God to manifest his displeasure against it. On the other hand, the mind of man, only partially acquainted with the punishment of fallen angels, was prepared to receive the impression of the sacrifice of Christ as something perfectly novel and strange: nothing, therefore, could be more fitted to display to angels and men the true deformity of sin, and the immaculate holiness of God.

The relation of Christ to the Father also supplies us with another view of this subject. It is not unlikely that there are created beings who are as much superior to man as he is to the lowest reptiles, and to whom the perdition of the human race would have been of no greater comparative importance than the destruction of an ant-hill, and its inhabitants, to us. From the Creator we are certainly far more remote in the scale of being, than the meanest animalcule is from man. Yet our insignificancy did not secure us from punishment; and so awful an evil was our guilt, little as we are, that the only mode of expiating it was the gift of the only begotten Son of God, to assume our mean condition, and to bear in his person the penalty which we had deserved. Mercy could not be shown to man, except at the expense of God's beloved Son. It is impossible to say, whether this sacrifice displayed more fully the divine benevolence, or the divine purity. The gift of such an expiatory sacrifice exhibits the one, and the necessity of it evidences the other. And here I cannot but remark, though it does not properly belong to this part of the subject, that God's glory, as a moral Governor, could not have been so prominently brought out in any other way. Unmingled justice could not have been impeached; but it is in the union of attributes so apparently irreconcilable as primitive justice and infinite benevolence, that the entire Deity, so to speak, is presented to the view of the universe. The wisdom which arrayed, the power which overruled, the fidelity which consummated such a scheme, are all worthy of God; and each of these attributes, in such a mode of display, is not only reflective of the divine glory, but highly conducive to the moral advantage of the intelligent creation.

It is proper that I should remind you of the distinction between those evils which naturally result from sin, and the direct inflictions of the judgments of God. It is certain, that some forms of misery are directly and essentially connected with transgression, apart from all distinct divine appointment. Thus, such passions as envy and malice necessarily render the individual unhappy who is under their influence; and if God exerted no moral superintendence over his creatures, their effect would be the same. An envious and malignant spirit could not be otherwise than unhappy. Now, evils of this class, though they are sure indications of the pernicious character of sin, cannot be regarded as evidences of the divine purity; and their prevalence can, of consequence, reflect no glory upon God. Had man been given over to perdition, as the result of his offences, these would, without doubt, have formed no inconsiderable portion of his misery. It is, indeed, terrible to reflect upon the wretchedness of a soul given over to the unrestricted dominion of turbulent and ungratified passion. But we cannot conceive of such a being as conducing directly to the divine honour, except so far as he was the subject of positive infliction from the justice of God; and the design of God's rectoral superintendence could have been only partially accomplished in the everlasting condemnation of the human race. But in the case of Christ's vicarious sufferings, we perceive that they resulted directly from the infliction of divine justice. In him there was no irregular passion, or unsubdued appetite, to augment his sorrow. Against any such aggravation he was secured by the most immaculate purity. Hence all that he endured was the distinct demonstration of the divine purity. The being who suffered was the object of the divine regard and affection in the highest degree; and this assures us, that on him the rod would fall as lightly as possible. And yet, insignificant as were the creatures whose penalty he had to endure, perfectly holy as was his nature and his life, beloved as he was by his Father, yet so determined was the divine abhorrence of sin, that his sufferings transcended human conception, and caused his nature to shrink from the dreadful trial. Nothing can be more simple, or more solemn, than the sacred history on this subject. The trouble of soul, the heavy amazement, the sweat of blood, the ministering angel, the intolerable sorrow of the cross:—all are brought before us with so great clearness and vividness, that he must indeed have a most insensible spirit who can read the record without a distinct and an awful impression of the divine purity. Reflect, my dear friend, I beseech you, upon the prayer, "If it be possible, let this cup pass from me: nevertheless not as I will, but as thou wilt." (Matt. xxvi. 39.) Turn over its import in your mind. Meditate on the infinite resources of divine wisdom; and then ask your own heart to what conclusion you ought to come from the fact, that it was not possible that this cup should pass from the lips of the spotless Saviour. Is not this, indeed, the most magnificent, and yet the most dreadful, demonstration of the righteousness God?

But, beyond this, it will occur to you, that no illustration of the perfection of God's government could be exclusively penal. The ends of justice are answered by the punishment of sin: but, for their full accomplishment, the reward of virtue and obedience is equally necessary. Had the human race personally endured the penalty due to their transgression, there could have been no administration of reward; and, however severe such an infliction would have been, it would have evidenced nothing more than that God hated sin. But it was desirable, if not necessary, that his delight in goodness should have been equally apparent. And this could only have been effected by the vicarious suffering of Christ. Christ himself is rewarded by the highest exaltation in the universe. To him is given universal dominion: on his head are many crowns; and to him every intelligent creature must, sooner or later, render his homage. Such is the reward of that "servant" of God "in whom he delighted;" and such is the evidence which is supplied to us of the infinite complacency with which the Sovereign of all regards obedience. But, beyond this, God, for Christ's sake, has engaged to extend untold blessings to all who believe. In such he now delights, and "it doth not yet appear what they shall be." God has resolved to employ eternity in displaying his infinite delight in souls purchased and cleansed by the blood of Christ; and while his judgments shall only be commensurate with the guilt of the finally impenitent, his blessings upon the redeemed shall infinitely transcend, not their merit only, but their most exalted conception.

Such is the glory which the vicarious sacrifice of Christ reflects upon God. It is not enough to say, that the ends of justice are more fully answered in this respect than they could have been by the destruction of the human race, and the accumulation of the most dreadful calamities upon our earth and its sons for ever and ever. There is indeed no language which we can employ which will adequately represent the glory of the evangelical scheme. The glimpses which our partial knowledge of its facts afford us may well ravish our affections and admiration; and with infinitely greater emphasis than could be supplied by the mere survey of creation, we are compelled to exclaim, "What is man, that thou art thus mindful of him, or the son of man, that thou thus visitest him?"

The consideration of the second part of this subject I must postpone till my next letter.

Letter XII.

My dear Friend,

I now resume the subject partially considered in my last letter. I there endeavoured to show that, as far as the ends of justice directly respected God, they were more fully accomplished by the vicarious suffering of Christ, than they could have been by the actual punishment of offending man. The other design of legislation and government, to which I proposed to direct your attention, is, the encouragement of obedience, and the prevention of crime; and this, I wish to prove, is also more perfectly provided for in the atonement, than by the direct infliction of the penalty of the law.

What effect might have been produced upon the higher orders of God's creatures, by the eternal misery of the human race, we are not informed. We have an intimation, in the last verses of the prophecy of Isaiah, that, upon the completion of the present divine economy, the punishment of the wicked shall be a subject of universal and eternal contemplation; and that the spectacle shall produce a permanent impression of the loathsomeness of sin. Some such influence the destruction of mankind might perhaps have exerted upon the rest of the creation who witnessed it; but beyond this no analogy is sufficient to carry us. Of the effect which such an inevitable doom would have had upon man himself, our acquaintance with human nature enables us to speak with more confidence.

And here let me remind you, that our argument regards man in his lapsed and depraved condition. If it be true, which I suppose you admit, that man is by nature corrupted and sinful, it is equally true, that all restoring influence must come from without. The notion of inherent retrievableness cannot consist with the condition of a totally fallen creature. And yet it must be by some such influence that evil is repressed, and goodness encouraged. In fact, the very possibility of avoiding sin and embracing virtue, must have its source in that which is extrinsic of man's natural character. Now the Scriptures uniformly ascribe this influence to the Holy Spirit of God: the question, therefore, simply is, whether man, in a condition of condemnation, is capable of commanding this sanctifying agency. That he cannot on the ground of merit, is obvious; that he should have any appeal to the mercy of God, is unreasonable. The very fact of his condemnation, legally considered, cuts him off from all such resources. It follows, therefore, that he must remain destitute of any restoring power, except upon the supposition that such power was in no way connected with the divine authority and administration; which is absurd. To this conclusion, I think, we could have no difficulty in coming, apart from all direct testimony of the Scriptures.

But we are not left to grope our way by any mere abstract reasoning. The Bible sets the question fully at rest. The gift of the Holy Spirit is the immediate result of the mediation of Christ. See Acts ii. 33, *et al. freq.* To this gift, therefore, the mediation of Christ is necessary; and as this results, from his expiatory sacrifice, it follows, that, had there been no such sacrifice, the influences of the blessed Spirit could not have been vouchsafed to man. The human race, therefore, might have been punished; but their punishment would have failed to secure those divine communications by which alone they could have shunned the evil, and secured the purity, of which the divine law testifies. Apart from the atonement, we are doomed to a condition of perpetuated depravity, of hopeless and impotent sinfulness.

But by the vicarious and meritorious suffering of Christ, every barrier to our partaking of the restoring grace of the Spirit is removed; and the gift of blessing is therefore made matter of distinct provision in the covenant of the Gospel. The energy of the Spirit's influence, which we may partake, is not limited, except by our necessity; and the method for securing it is as simple and easy as its effect is delightful. The instruction, the conviction, the guidance, the adopting, the sealing, the comforting, the sanctifying, of the Spirit, are each and all ensured to us by the most clear and specific promises; and it may be safely affirmed, that, unless God had withdrawn the power of moral agency from man, he could not have more amply provided for his deliverance from pollution, than he has by the gift of the Holy Ghost, through the expiatory work of Christ.

It is to be remarked, also, that, in the absence of the atonement, man would have been destitute of adequate motive to attempt to obey the divine law. Suppose the irrevocable sentence of condemnation to be suspended over the whole human race, and what would be the result? Spirits of the more gentle and yielding order would become the victims of the most oppressive apprehension. Every energy would be paralysed beyond recovery; and they would sink down into the most abject and pitiable despair. Minds of a more heroic cast would harden themselves against all moral impression, and would seek forgetfulness of their doom in the recklessness of vice. Human effort must be sustained by hope; and if it be utterly destroyed, it is vain to expect anything resembling energy. It follows, therefore, that the consciousness of unavoidable destruction, instead of encouraging, would have repressed, every attempt at virtue, and would rather have tended to the increase, than the prevention, of sin.

Nor can this argument be evaded by the supposition, that men might have been left in ignorance of their certain destiny; or even that they might have been once more placed under a legal dispensation, and informed upon the subject of the sanctions by which the law is accompanied; for, to say nothing of the absence of the restoring energy of God, which is essential to the purity of a depraved spirit, the want of any adequate moral motive would have been sufficient to render such an arrangement unprofitable. For, what motive does the law supply to a fallen spirit that could excite and sustain the practice of piety? "Obey and live; transgress and die," is the language of the law; and he must be indeed desperately insensible to the real character of man, who supposes this sufficient to secure his obedience. Look at the melancholy picture—a picture as true as it is melancholy—which St. Paul gives in the seventh chapter of the Epistle to the Romans, of the unavailing attempts of an unrenewed mind to submit itself to the law. Observe, too, that, in the case which he supposes, there is a distinct admission of the sanctity, the justice, and even the beneficial character of the law, and an inward approbation of its dictates. But, spite of all, the power of nature, being destitute of any counterpoise of prevalent moral motive, overcomes good resolution, and general virtuous inclination. And if this be the fact, where there is so much that is estimable and auxiliary to virtue, what would be the condition of the mass of mankind, in whom there is neither approval of the law, nor even perception of its real character?

The Judaical dispensation was probably designed to instruct mankind in the utter inefficiency of a merely legal economy; for, though it was not exclusively legal, as its sacrifices testify, yet it presented the law to the eyes of the Jews with peculiar prominence, and demanded their obedience on strictly legal grounds. But that it was inadequate to its proposed design is evident, not only from historical facts, but from the distinct testimony of the New Testament writers. St. Paul, in writing to the Galatians, speaks of the Jewish church as in a state of minority, and the law, he says, was its schoolmaster,—leader of children,—to bring us to Christ; not only because it could not justify, but also because it was unable to secure the obedience of those subjected to it. By this "experiment," if it may be so called, God, therefore, testified to all ages, that a legal covenant was unsuitable to the condition of man; and thus reproved self-righteous human nature, which would fain derive from itself all the spiritual good which it requires.

On the other hand, the atonement of Christ supplies the most ample motives, as well as the most desirable facilities, to obedience. I have already shown that it furnishes the most impressive views of the divine holiness, and the most irrefragable evidence of the severity and inflexibility of the divine law. Now, consider what would be its probable practical influence in this light. To a mind properly enlightened and impressed, it is not too much to say, that it would do far more to deter from sin than any other conceivable revelation. Let me appeal to your own mind in proof of this assertion. What grandeur and breadth is there in the divine law, as illustrated by the sufferings of Christ! What awful and inflexible purity in the divine mind! Above all, how is the certainty and the terror of the punishment of the impenitent enhanced by this solemn exhibition! "He spared not his own Son." This is at once an answer to all temptations to unbelief. The minister of the legal covenant stood on Horeb, and beheld the idolatry of the seed of the promise: Christ looks from Calvary, and sees his church in the deepest sorrow, astonishment, and awe.

The doctrine of the Apostle Paul, in the eighth of Romans, is most apposite to this subject. He thus expresses it, verses 3, "For what the law could not do" by its sanction, "in that it was weak through" "the corruptness of "the flesh," shown in the preceding chapter, "God" hath done, by "sending his own Son, in the likeness of sinful flesh," as our teacher and example; "and for sin," that is, for a sin-offering, "hath condemned sin in the flesh," that is, given an evidence of the guiltiness of sin far beyond what the law could effect, by inflicting upon Christ in human nature the punishment due to human guilt, "that the righteousness" enjoined in, or the righteousness "of, the law might be fulfilled in"—by— "us, who walk not after the flesh, but after the Spirit." I cannot, of course, say how this passage may affect your mind; but to me, I confess, it supplies the strongest confirmation of the general views contained in this and in my last letter. The inefficiency of the law is attributed to the depraved condition of human nature. Such is the blindness of the mind, such the insensibility of the heart, and such the depravity of the inclinations, of man, that no legal enactment or condemnation, even if it were that of all mankind, could succeed in producing the impression of the purity of its nature, or in securing human obedience. But, to remedy this inadequacy of everything legal, God sent his Son, and caused him to possess the actual nature which had sinned, and in this nature to become a vicarious sacrifice. Thus did he exhibit the purity of his nature and government, and evidence the certainty of the condemnation of all who adhered to their sin. And all this was done that we might be supplied with that degree of moral motive, and of the Spirit's influence, by which we should be enabled to fulfil the righteousness of the law. This, as I understand it, is the meaning of the passage; and, unless I am greatly deceived, you will find it very difficult to discover any other consistent interpretation: and if this exposition be allowed, I need not add, that the position is fully made out,—that the vicarious sacrifice of Christ promotes the ends of divine justice more completely than any conceivable arrangement of a merely legal or primitive character.

Before I dismiss the subject of motive, as connected with the atonement of Christ, I must not omit to remark, that there is supplied through it the noblest incentive to piety and obedience of which the mind of man is capable,—an incentive which, in generosity and elevation, infinitely transcends even that revelation of the divine purity which is, through the agency of the Spirit, so powerful in deterring from sin: I mean, the love of God shed abroad in the heart, through the Holy Ghost given unto us. The Apostle Paul describes its necessity and its excellence, 1 Cor. xiii. The Apostle John teaches us its origin: "We love him because he first loved us." (1 John iv. 19.) The lives of the first Christians exhibit its energy; and our acquaintance with human nature assures us, that beyond this there is no higher moral impulse. Command his love, and you have the man; and surely the love of Christ to us, in his vicarious sufferings, is, above all other things, infinitely energetic to the production of reciprocated affection. This is the true secret of Christian conduct.

"Talk they of morals? O thou bleeding Love,
The best morality is love of thee."

"God is love; and he that dwelleth in love dwelleth in God, and God in him." It is this which will sustain when all other supports fail; and when the heart is fully imbued with its spirit, it will turn away from all the fascinations of that which is sensual and earthly. Learn the loftiest virtue; and enjoy the liveliest hope.

> "Thenceforth, all world's desire will in thee die,
>   And all earth's glory, on which men do gaze,
> Seem dirt and dross in thy pure-sighted eye,
>   Compared to that celestial beauty's blaze
>   Whose glorious beams all fleshly sense doth daze
> With admiration of their passing light,
> Blinding the eyes, and 'lumining the spright.
>
> "Then shall thy ravish'd soul inspired be
>   With heavenly thoughts, far above human skill,
> And thy bright radiant eyes shall plainly see
>   The Idea of His pure glory, present still
>   Before thy face, that all thy spirit shall fill
> With sweet enragement of celestial love,
> Kindled through sight of those fair things above."
>
> Spenser's Hymn to Heavenly Love.

These views, I trust, will enable you to discern that, apart from the direct consideration of the happiness of the human race, there is an infinite fitness in the vicarious suffering of Christ. It has sometimes been urged as an objection to this doctrine, that if man were so totally alienated from God as we represent him, there was nothing in his condition to move the exercise of the divine love towards him. This argument has been supposed to have a double force: it is thought to prove, that, if God's love was thus moved towards us, our condition could not have been so depraved as we affirm; otherwise, it is argued, as the divine love is regulated by his wisdom and purity, our entire sinfulness must have for ever repelled, instead of invited, the regard of God. But, for a moment admitting this to be true, it is, I think, sufficiently clear, from what has before been remarked, that the atonement of Christ promotes in so extraordinary a degree the glory of the divine government, and so impressively illustrates the divine character, that this alone would be sufficient to move the divine wisdom. Indeed, it is difficult to reconcile to our notions of God's perfections, the withholding of a scheme so fraught with honour to himself, and producing practical results so singularly desirable to all pure beings. This view detracts nothing from the divine compassion: since, after all, the happiness and salvation of man was the obvious consequence. But as every other method of administration would have been infinitely inferior in its moral influence upon God's government, no argument against it can by possibility be founded upon the unfitness of man to call forth the divine regard. We may with all reverence affirm, that God owed it to his own nature to originate the atonement of Christ; and for aught we know to the contrary, there may be countless multitudes of the highest created intelligences, whose wisdom and happiness are so enhanced by the work of Christ and its results, that their advantage might also have moved the Governor of all thus to bless and ennoble his human family.

Another class of objectors to the doctrine of the atonement have urged the insignificance of the human race, as an argument against its reasonableness and probability. It is not to be supposed, we are told, that, amidst the splendour of the universe, and the multitude of its suns and systems, a point so extremely small as our earth should be the object of such a profusion of mercy, and such a magnificent scheme of benevolence. But you will readily perceive that this objection results from a partial view of the subject. To give it any weight, it must be shown that the benefits of Christ's suffering are wholly confined to the human race; that it reflects no considerable honour upon the divine character, and affords no moral influence to the superior beings who dwell more immediately in the divine presence. But as this can never be proved, because certainly untrue, it follows that there is no cogency in such a method of reasoning. If it were possible that some extraordinary exertion of the power of God in the behalf of the meanest insect could enhance, in a proportionate degree, the honour of the divine government, it would certainly be proper that such a dispensation should take place. It is the greatness and honour of the Creator which gives force to the argument; and so long as this is eminently secured, the insignificancy of the creature cannot at all derogate from its worth.

In fact, when we come to examine the subject more minutely, the insignificance of man, instead of being an objection to the doctrine under consideration, is no inconsiderable presumption in its favour. It is certain that this fact gives that peculiar character to the work of Christ, which supplies so strong an evidence of its divine appointment. It is this which so strikingly enhances the benevolence and condescension of the interposition of God in our behalf. Had Christ taken upon him the nature of angels, to win back to virtue and obedience the sublime apostates of that race, the fact could not and would not have been dwelt on with that admiring love which the actual incarnation almost forces from the mind which contemplates it; and hence there would have been by no means that extensive moral advantage which is the result of the atonement for man.

It is also worthy of your attention, that the results, as they respect the vindication and illustration of the divine character and administration, are infinitely superior in the substitution of Christ for guilty man, to those of a scheme for the salvation of higher beings. The sin of a more exalted race appears to us to possess a peculiar aggravation of guilt, and no argument, nor illustration of the heinousness of their offence, seems to be required. It was sufficient that they should personally endure the penalty due to their transgression; and the infliction of this, in proportion to the excellence of their natures, was a sufficient demonstration of the divine righteousness. Now, though the insignificancy of the human race could not be supposed capable of shielding them from the punishment of sin, it might have been supposed that it would have precluded the necessity of any peculiar exhibition of the divine abhorrence. But when, in order to our redemption, the Son of God became incarnated, and was subjected to the agony of the cross, the impression of the infinite purity of the divine nature became unspeakably more deep and vivid than it otherwise could have been. The exquisite sensibility and inflexible justice of the law was splendidly manifested; and it is now obvious to all, both in heaven and on earth, that sin, mean as may be its agent or victim, is, in every degree, and throughout all generations, the object of the divine abhorrence; and that the guilt of sin, even in the lowest rational creatures, is so tremendous as to make the most exalted of beings tremble and writhe under the oppression of its weight and curse. With what awful reverence, with what solemn delight, would such illustrations of the divine perfections inspire all pure minds! The songs of heaven might well be supposed under their influence to assume a deeper tone, and the spirits of angels to catch a more powerful inspiration of the divine character. Love would beget love; and the unveiling of the holiness of God in the work of redemption, would kindle the noblest ambition in the noblest of all creatures. Such we know is the case with the human mind when brought under the due impression of the subject; and such, in a far higher degree, we judge by analogy, is likely to happen in the best born of the family of God.

You well know how the microscopic kingdom affects a reflecting mind. Men who look with little emotion upon the stateliness of the horse, or the fleetness of the antelope, are smitten with wonder to perceive the array of sensation and instinct, combined with the most perfect muscular machinery, in beings that people the world of a single drop of water; and I think it will be difficult to repress a degree of religious emotion at such discoveries, however little disposition there may ordinarily be towards feelings of that order. It appears, therefore, as if the discovery of the divine operation was impressive in an inverse ratio to the importance of the beings for whose benefit it is employed; as if the very remoteness of any objects from our own rank, rendered the perfections of God exhibited in them more conspicuous and illustrious. It is probable that this is a law of all created natures; and the more insignificant, therefore, we conceive ourselves to be, the more admirably adapted is the vicarious suffering of Christ to impress the highest of God's creatures with an increasing sense of the glory and perfection of the eternal Mind.

Letter XIII.

My dear Friend,

I suppose you will readily admit, that, in order to give effect to any arrangement not directly provided for in the constitution of a law, the consent of the authority from which that law emanated must necessarily be secured. The importance that there should be every requisite evidence of such consent, is also manifest; since, whatever practical good is contemplated, it must depend upon the degree of certainty and validity associated with such an arrangement. In the case before us, indeed, we may go further, and say, that any extra-legal dispensation must be matter of direct divine origination and appointment; as it is revolting to our notions of the perfections of God, that he should receive suggestions from his creatures as to the principles of his moral government. The degree of practical good resulting from any special measure of the divine administration, must, in a very peculiar way, depend upon the nature of the evidence by which it is confirmed. And, as our apprehension of abstract fitness, and of the general modes of God's operation, is exceedingly faint, it is also necessary that such evidence should be remarkably palpable and varied; that thus even the feeblest mind might perceive its force, and that every peculiarity of human scepticism might be provided against, and left without apology.

Now, what are the facts? Nothing is more evident from the Scriptures, than that the mission and work of Jesus is exclusively of divine origination and appointment. In fact, we cannot conceive of any created mind being capable of conjecturing so stupendous a scheme of wisdom and benevolence. The scepticism upon the doctrine of the atonement which prevails among those professed Christians who trust to the exertion of their own reason for ascertaining divine truth, is an evidence of the insufficiency of the human mind, not only to suggest such a system, but even, when left to itself, to admit it when revealed. Were the mind of man the proper gauge of the character and perfections of God, this scepticism might startle and infect us; but when an alleged inquiry into truth is conducted upon a principle so monstrous, the rejection of any doctrine is rather a presumption in favour of its divine origin, than any argument against it.

And the testimony of Scripture is not only most explicit as to the divine origin of Christ's expiatory work, but equally so as to the acceptableness of the manner in which he performed that work. Hence once and again, during his public ministry, did the Father testify from heaven his complacent regards towards the person and labours of Christ. And now that the work of Christ has been completed, we have such a concurrence of testimony, as to the acceptance of his mediation, as is sufficient to satisfy every candid mind. Into the nature and force of this evidence, we may profitably inquire a little more at large.

The first evidence in the order of time is the resurrection of Christ from the dead. I shall not now go into the consideration of the credibility of this miracle; as upon that subject, I presume, you are already informed and satisfied. But suffer me to offer a few remarks upon the importance which we ought to attach to it. In the first place, it illustrates, in a striking manner, the harmony of counsel and operation between Christ and the Father. Thus, it is in some cases represented as effected by the power of the Father, while in other instances it is directly attributed to Christ. Passages of the former class are exceedingly numerous. The latter view is supplied in John ii. 19: "Jesus answered and said unto them, Destroy this temple, and in three days I will raise it up." (See verses 21, 22.) And again in the passage which I quoted in a former letter, "I lay down my life that I might take it again. I have power to lay it down, and I have power to take it again." (John x. 17, 18.) And lest there should be any hesitation as to the nature and extent of this power, we find the Scriptures representing it as vested in Christ, in his mediatorial character, without any limitation. Thus, John v. 21, 26: "As the Father raiseth up the dead, and quickeneth them; even so the Son quickeneth whom he will." "For as the Father hath life in himself; so hath he given to the Son to have life in himself." And again, John xi. 25: "Jesus said unto her, I am the resurrection, and the life: he that believeth in me, though he were dead, yet shall he live." This harmony of counsel and operation between the Father and the Mediator supplies satisfactory evidence of the complacency with which the mediatorial work was contemplated by God, and confirms and illustrates the ample declaration of Christ himself, John viii. 29: "He that sent me is with me: the Father hath not left me alone; for I do always those things that please him."

In the second place, it is to be remarked that the resurrection is not a single and isolated miracle, but is essentially connected with all that is vital in Christianity. I do not merely mean on account of its evidence to the divinity of Christ's claims, but also as it is the source of the general system of mediatorial arrangement and blessings. Upon this you will find that the preaching of the Apostles was founded, and to it they attributed the gifts which Christ in his mediatorial character dispensed, especially, the gift of pardon. Thus the Apostle Paul, preaching at Antioch, deduces this cheering doctrine from his preceding discourse on the resurrection: "Be it known unto you, therefore, men and brethren, that through this man is preached unto you the forgiveness of sins:" (Acts xiii. 38:) a sentiment which he confirms Romans iv. 25, where he expressly declares, that Christ "was delivered for our offences, and raised again for our justification." The resurrection and glorification of the bodies of believers is attributed to that of Christ; and this is the consummation of the mediatorial work. (See 1 Cor. xv. *passim.*) The Apostle Paul also makes the resurrection of Christ the pledge whereby God assures mankind that by him the world shall be judged: "Because he hath appointed a day, in the which he will judge the world in righteousness by that man whom he hath ordained; whereof he hath given assurance unto all men, in that he hath raised him from the dead." (Acts xvii. 31.)

Closely connected with the resurrection, is the exaltation of Christ. That this partakes of the nature of a reward, I endeavoured to show in a former letter. And if this be the fact, it is scarcely possible for us to be supplied with more abundant evidence of the approbation with which the Father contemplates the vicarious suffering of the Son. Still further: if this reward consist of, or is inseparably associated with, a covenant of mercy and benevolence, the proof rises to the highest clearness of which it is capable. Every blessing dispensed through the medium of this covenant, becomes in itself an evidence that the sacrifice of Christ is perfectly and for ever acceptable to God. But what need of multiplying proof on this subject? The question may be resolved into a simple inquiry as to the efficacy of the evangelical scheme of salvation. For if the soul of one sinful man has ever been sanctified, and then received to share the blessings of paradise, there cannot remain the slightest doubt as to the prevalency of the work of Christ, and the complacency with which God contemplates it. It is enough. "After this I beheld," says St. John, "and, lo, a great multitude, which no man could number, of all nations, and kindreds, and people, and tongues, stood before the throne, and before the Lamb, clothed with white robes, and palms in their hands; and cried with a loud voice, saying, Salvation to our God which sitteth upon the throne, and unto the Lamb. And all the angels stood round about the throne, and about the elders and the four beasts, and fell before the throne on their faces, and worshipped God, saying, Amen: Blessing, and glory, and wisdom, and thanksgiving, and honour, and power, and might, be unto our God for ever and ever. Amen. And one of the elders answered, saying unto me, What are these which are arrayed in white robes? and whence came they? And I said unto him, Sir, thou knowest. And he said to me, These are they which came out of great tribulation, and have washed their robes, and made them white in the blood of the Lamb. Therefore are they before the throne of God, and serve him day and night in his temple: and he that sitteth on the throne shall dwell among them. They shall hunger no more, neither thirst any more; neither shall the sun light on them, nor any heat. For the Lamb which is in the midst of the throne shall feed them, and shall lead them unto living fountains of waters: and God shall wipe away all tears from their eyes." (Rev. vii. 9-17.) Such testimonies as these are evidently sufficient to prove that God has accepted the vicarious suffering of Christ as an ample satisfaction to his insulted justice and violated law. We should do the subject great injustice, however, to leave it in this position. I have, I hope, made it manifest that the atonement is inconceivably more honourable to God, than any actual penal infliction upon offending man. The question, therefore, more properly is, Has God acknowledged the vicarious work of his Son, in all its copiousness of merit; and do the Scriptures supply us with evidence that the blessings resulting from it are proportionably great and eminent? Does the atonement effect more than could have been effected by any mere legal arrangement; and, supposing man to have been rewarded for a spotless obedience to the divine law, have we reason to believe that his condition would have been less desirable than that in which he will ultimately be placed by the influence of the merit of Christ? This, I think you will perceive, is important to the harmony of the doctrine under consideration; and even if I should not succeed in demonstrating that such is the fact, it will be interesting to discover a strong probability of its being so.

I need not say that the difficulty in this train of reasoning will principally arise from our utter ignorance of the blessings in reversion for man if he had not sinned. The Scriptures, as far as direct testimony is concerned, are quite silent upon this subject; and for this there is no doubt that a sufficient reason might be assigned, though this is not the place to pursue an inquiry into it. Yet I think it not unreasonable to deduce a conclusion even from the silence of the word of God, since it can hardly be supposed that the mere legal reward of unsinning man could have been of a transcendently glorious order, without some reference having been made to such a fact. In addition to this, the terms of Adam's original trial seem to suggest to us that he was rather to be moved by the apprehension of punishment, than inspired by the hope of reward, which it is hardly probable would have been the case, had the reward to be secured by his obedience been of so exalted a character as to have exerted any very powerful moral influence over him. At all events, I think it may rationally be believed, that unsinning human nature would have retained the same relation of inferiority to more exalted intelligences, even in a state of reward, as in a state of trial. These, I grant, are but conjectures, and I therefore do not insist upon them, except so far as their probability may seem to warrant their admission. If, however, it can be shown that the blessings procured by Christ are of the most exalted nature of which we can conceive, and if it can be rendered probable that the station to be occupied by glorified human nature is indeed more perfect and honourable than that for which he was at the creation qualified, it may be fairly presumed that God's approbation of the mediatorial scheme is more decisive and ample than would have been his complacency in unsinning man.

The *à priori* argument is, I think, most conclusive; namely, that as Christ has more fully honoured the divine government than could have been effected by anything merely legal, therefore God must more fully approve of his work. Or, to give it another form: as Christ was a being of infinite dignity, and as his sacrifice, by its perfect spontaneity, was infinitely meritorious, therefore, the divine respect towards it must be infinitely complacent. But our present inquiry, you will perceive, directly regards the harmony of the doctrine; and is, in simple terms, What evidence has God supplied of his acknowledgment of Christ's infinite and transcendent virtue? or, Are the blessings thus secured to the human race equal to a proof of God's transcendent approbation of it, and delight in it?

The first fact which I wish you to notice, in reply to this inquiry, is the exaltation of human nature, in the person of Christ, to the highest dignity of which we can conceive. He sat down on the right hand of the Majesty in the heavens, "far above all principality, and power, and might, and dominion, and every name that is named, not only in this world, but also in that which is to come." (Eph. i. 21.) To Christ, in this nature, universal homage is to be paid, every enemy is to be subdued, and everlasting dominion is to belong. Consider, then, the views of the capacities of our nature supplied by such testimonies. We have no idea of the human body, except as gross and frail; to the strength and fleetness of which, the brute creation offers many examples of superiority. We are scarcely capable of conceiving of it otherwise than as a hinderance to the operations of the spirit. Nothing, indeed, can be more humiliating, than the constant clog which an ardent mind feels upon its movements in the dulness and feebleness of its material organization. But here we see a human body so changed, refined, and glorified, as to be fitted to sit upon the divine throne, excelling in beauty the ethereal vehicles of the highest order of created beings, and taking its rank accordingly. What must be the perfection of a body which is capable of sustaining a glory too exalted to be contemplated by us in our present condition without instant death? What must be that vigour, and what that immortal elasticity, which shall never know fatigue; senses which shall never seek or need repose; youth that shall never require renovation? Contemplate, too, the exaltation of that human mind which shall, in union with the Godhead, be capable of exerting unlimited power, and so extending its triumph as to bless with immortal joy every creature who comes under its benign dominion; a mind incapable of perplexity, doubt, or darkness; unacquainted with either sorrow or disturbance; filled with immortal truth; flashing its radiance upon the fairest intellects, till their light grows dim in its ray; and sending forth the long lines of its glory to the utmost limit of thought and being. Such is the human nature of Christ; and such, in a smaller degree, is the glory which shall certainly be bestowed upon his saints. Our vile bodies (how truly vile are they in the comparison!) are to be fashioned after the similitude of his glorious body, according to that resistless energy by which hereafter he shall subdue all things to himself.

Consider also the relation which Christ, in his mediatorial glory, sustains to his people. In the connexion of the passage just quoted, the Apostle, having spoken of the exaltation of Christ, adds, that God "hath put all things under his feet, and given him to be the head over all things to the church," which is "the fulness of Him that filleth all in all." (Ephes. i. 22, 23.) Again, in the Epistle to the Hebrews: "Both he that sanctifieth and they who are sanctified are all of one" nature, as the foregoing and succeeding part of the chapter proves: "for which cause he is not ashamed to call them brethren." (Heb. ii. 11.) When the Apostle Paul speaks of the advantage of God's gracious predestination, he describes it as the being "conformed to the image of his Son, that he might be the first-born among many brethren." (Rom. viii. 29.) The same writer, representing the connexion between the resurrection of Christ and that of his people, speaks of the one as the first-fruits; and goes on to remark, that the resemblance of the saints to Christ shall be in effect analogous to the resemblance of the natural man to Adam. "But now is Christ risen from the dead, and become the first-fruits of them that slept." (1 Cor. xv. 20.) "And so it is written, The first man Adam was made a living soul; the last Adam was made a quickening spirit. Howbeit that was not first which is spiritual, but that which is natural; and afterward that which is spiritual. The first man is of the earth, earthy: the second man is the Lord from heaven. As is the earthy, such are they also that are earthy: and as is the heavenly, such are they also that are heavenly.

And as we have borne the image of the earthy, we shall also bear the image of the heavenly." (1 Cor. xv. 45-49.) Nothing can more strongly indicate the glory which the redeemed shall share in the day of resurrection, than the phraseology here employed, "As is the earthy, such are they also that are earthy: and as is the heavenly, such are they also that are heavenly." Each, οιος, in perfect conformity to its proper type; therefore, in perfect conformity to the heavenly body of Christ. And, καθως, like as, we have borne, ταν εικονα, the image, the exact resemblance, of Adam, so shall we bear the exact resemblance, the image, of Christ, the heavenly One, ταν εικονα του επουρανιου. Another passage is still more conclusive: "To him that overcometh will I grant to sit with me in my throne, even as I also overcame, and am set down with my Father in his throne." (Rev. iii. 21.)

Remark, too, the dignity which men are to sustain in the closing acts of the mediatorial kingdom. The disciples were distinctly promised that, in the great day of retribution, they should have the glory of subordinate judges in that most august of courts. And the Apostle Paul carries the view out still further in the first Epistle to the Corinthians, vi. 2, 3: "Do ye not know that the saints shall judge the world? and if the world shall be judged by you, are ye unworthy to judge the smallest matters? Know ye not that we shall judge angels? how much more things that pertain to this life?" This subject, you will readily perceive, might be pursued at great length; but it is not necessary. The passages which I have quoted, I think, amount to the proof that human nature is destined to sustain the first rank in the creation of God. Thus, in those visions of God in which we seem to have the largest insight into the constitution of the heavenly state, we have the angelic host standing in all their multitude before the glory of the throne. The following is the magnificent description of the Prophet Daniel:— "The Ancient of days did sit, whose garment was white as snow, and the hair of his head like the pure wool: his throne was like the fiery flame, and his wheels as burning fire. A fiery stream issued and came forth from before him: thousand thousands ministered unto him, and ten thousand times ten thousand stood before him." (Dan. vii. 9, 10.) Now turn to Revelation iv. 3, 4, for a description somewhat different: "And he that sat" on the throne "was to look upon like a jasper and a sardine stone: and there was a rainbow round about the throne, in sight like unto an emerald;" the emblem of covenant and grace. "And round about the throne were four and twenty thrones, θρονοι: and upon the thrones I saw four-and-twenty elders sitting, clothed in white raiment: and they had on their heads crowns of gold." I suppose I need not expatiate upon the significance of these crowned elders sitting upon a throne in a circle round the central throne. If there be any meaning at all in Scripture iconography, we are here taught the superiority of the representatives of the church, to all the other created inhabitants of heaven. The crown, the throne, the attitude, all impress us with this fact; and we must reject the emblems of the Bible altogether, if we do not concede thus much.

Now, whatever glory the nature of man is capable of attaining, or shall actually attain, all is attributed to the mediatorial triumphs of Christ. The passages which I have now quoted are conclusive upon this point. And since nothing of honour or enjoyment to be possessed by man is ascribed to any other source, the fair and legitimate conclusion is, that, apart from the atonement of Christ, he never could have attained this exaltation. Indeed it is utterly incredible that anything of mere legal meritoriousness could have ever raised the human race to the highest glory in the universe. It follows that the blessings secured to man by the vicarious work of Christ, very far transcend any which under the first covenant he could have attained. God has therefore acknowledged the infinite meritoriousness of the atonement, and has evidenced to his intelligent universe, that he accepts it as more honourable to his person and government than the unsinning obedience of any creature or any created race.

Letter XIV.

MY DEAR FRIEND,

IT MAY, PERHAPS, BE PROPER to remind you that I do not insist upon the suffering of Christ as being in any sense the same as the suffering of sinful man. I am not concerned to prove, what appears to me to be incapable of proof, that our Saviour actually endured in his own person the pains of damnation, nor that his sufferings amounted to the united punishment due to the whole human race. All that I contend for, is, that his passion was vicarious, that it was an ample satisfaction to the divine justice for human transgression, and that it was more illustrative of the designs of God's government than the actual perdition of the human race. It will follow, therefore, that God is by no means bound to dispense pardon and happiness to the whole of the human race. The meritoriousness of the atonement does not principally result from the intensity of the agony of Christ, but from those other considerations to which in former letters I directed your attention. Let the contrary be supposed, and you will at once discern how many errors may be successfully promulgated. For if Christ has endured all the pains which the human race can ever deserve, it will be most revolting to suppose that those pains should ever be repeated; and hence the salvation of all men becomes necessary. And this reasoning will apply to any degree of punitive infliction, as well as to that of eternal misery. For if all has been undergone which can ever be merited, any degree of further punishment is as unjust as, in its degree, would be eternal punishment. The scheme of universal restoration, therefore, will not at all relieve us from these absurdities; for no universalist is so infatuated as to suppose that the finally impenitent will escape every measure of suffering in the other world.

On the other hand, if it be supposed that Christ endured all that a certain part of the human race are capable of deserving, the perdition of that part is rendered for ever impossible; and if the suffering of Christ extends no farther, it is equally impossible that any other can be saved. I need not say that this opens the door to the most destructive Antinomianism, and therefore must be objectionable to all sober theologians. But if this be the fact, it goes directly to unweave the whole web of the argument by which the doctrine of the atonement is rendered consistent and credible. It is, in fact, after all, pardon and salvation by the divine prerogative; and, as far as discern, might be as readily achieved apart from the atonement, as in connexion with it. For if a certain proportion of the human race is to be raised to the enjoyment of heaven by the mere decree of God's eternal mercy, it is difficult to imagine what the satisfaction of the divine justice has to do with the arrangement. It may be said that the same decree which determined the end, determined also the means; but this will not evade the difficulty, except the appropriateness of the means can also be demonstrated. The appropriateness of the atonement, in our apprehension, results from its being an exhibition of the divine righteousness, and from its tendency to repress sin and encourage piety. But can that be a demonstration of the divine righteousness which renders it necessary that the larger proportion of mankind should continue in sin in this world, and be the inheritors of misery in the world to come? Can that be a demonstration of God's righteousness, which describes his regards as bestowed upon the human race irrespective of any moral fitness for his complacency? Can that be a demonstration of the divine righteousness, which is founded upon a mere arbitrary constitution of the will of God? If he could, by mere prerogative, decree that certain individuals should certainly be pardoned, is not the act of pardon, resulting originally from that decree, a mere act of prerogative also? And can that doctrine which represents the salvation of one and the perdition of another to be unavoidable, be said in any degree to minister to the moral advantage of the human race? Is it any evidence of the divine abhorrence of sin that he makes no sufficient provision for the deliverance of the majority of mankind from its influence? Can that view of the divine benevolence which restricts it to a few, prove a universal motive to obedience? If the inevitable perdition of the larger proportion of the human race is more honourable to God than their being placed in a salvable state, it is clear that the sacrifice of Christ is an inadequate exhibition of the divine purity, and that the government of God would have been more eminently illustrated by the perdition of the whole of Adam's posterity. But if, as I hope, I have shown the perdition of no human being is necessary to the vindication of the divine justice; if, indeed, this attribute is more fully vindicated by the suffering of Christ than it could have been by any penal infliction upon man; it would be most revolting to suppose that God should render unavoidable the eternal misery of any individual of our race. The vicarious suffering of Christ must, therefore, be sufficient to place all men in a salvable state; but, at the same time, could not have amounted to the pain which the whole of the human race might have deserved, since that would render necessary the salvation of all; which is absurd.

The only question, therefore, is, whether, besides those sufferings which Christ endured to place all men within the reach of mercy, he so fully submitted to the punishment which a few were capable of deserving, as to render their perdition impossible? In other words, are there some who must be saved, and others who will be saved? for it is mere mockery to say, that, of the vast multitudes of mankind, all of whom may be saved, not one will actually escape perdition. To this inquiry we might reply, "No; because compulsory holiness is not consistent with a state of probation;" but we prefer to answer, "No; because in the Scriptures the salvation of all is placed on the same footing." Thus, if it be true, that "whom he did foreknow, he also did predestinate to be conformed to the image of his Son, that he might be the first-born among many brethren," it is equally true, that them whom he did not know, he also did not predestinate; and whom he did not predestinate, them he also did not call, &c. Or, to give another form to the passage, All who are glorified have been justified, and all who are justified have been called, and all who are called have been predestinated to be conformed to the image of the Son, and all who are predestinated have been foreknown. (Rom. viii. 29, 30.) One scale is applicable to all who obtain salvation through Jesus Christ. Or suppose this not to be the fact, then shall we say that God glorifies some whom he does not justify? this is absurd; or, that he justifies some whom he does not call, who come to him without a call? this is impossible; or that he calls some whom he did not "predestinate to be conformed to the image of his Son?" but the calling is the result of predestination, and therefore it is unscriptural to suppose that the one ever exists without the other. Of course, all who are glorified have been foreknown, predestinated, called, and justified.

But there is yet another view of the subject, which is perhaps stronger; and that is, that the notion of the necessary salvation of some, and the possible salvation of others, is a derogation from the dignity and righteousness of God's government. For, surely, if all may be saved by the atonement, it is an unnecessary and injurious adjunct to that system to decree that some must be saved; for it is evident, that he who is saved, who may yet be lost, is a far more virtuous being than one who must be saved at all events. But it is the elect who are the objects of God's peculiar regard: that the whole of the Bible testifies. It follows, that the divine complacency does not depend upon the proportion of diligence in Christians, but upon a mere arbitrary and partial respect to individuals; which we know is not the fact. Besides, the notion of the unavoidableness of the salvation of some individuals, goes far to counteract the moral influence of the atonement. If the final happiness of these individuals is certainly secured, their employment of God's grace is also unavoidable. But an act which we cannot but perform, is no moral act at all. All such persons are therefore put beyond the capacity of honouring God. A mirror may just as well be said to honour the man whose features it correctly reflects, as that spirit to honour God which cannot be otherwise than conformed to his image. That process of grace, therefore, whereby a man is enabled to choose the divine service, and continue in it under the influence of moral motive, supplied by the atonement of Christ, and applied by the Holy Spirit, (which motive he is, nevertheless, capable of finally rejecting,)—such a process is more directly honourable to God's moral government in one single instance, than the compelled obedience of millions of beings, whose ultimate happiness they themselves can neither secure nor avert. If, therefore, it be admitted, that the atonement of Christ was designed at once to vindicate the divine righteousness, and to secure the largest possible amount of moral good to man, it will follow, that there can be no such thing as compulsory salvation, that all men may be saved, and that salvation may, nevertheless, be rejected by any.

If, therefore, the final destiny of man is to be determined by causes secondary to the atonement, the sufferings of Christ could, in no sense of the term, be those which the whole or any part of the human race would otherwise have endured for ever. Besides, in the nature of things, this appears impossible. For as it is not to be supposed that the Godhead of Christ was otherwise than impassible, his capacity of suffering must, after all have been that of human nature merely,—human nature, I admit, in a very high condition of energy and power, yet still but human nature. Of course, however great we consider his ability to have been, it must have had a certain limit. But we are incapable of conceiving any finite power capable of enduring, in a few hours, the accumulated miseries of countless millions of human spirits through unlimited duration,—spirits, too, strengthened and fitted for an immortality of undecaying wretchedness.

Besides, the very nature of the torments of hell precludes this notion. For beyond the direct infliction of the divine wrath, there is the withdrawal both of divine consolation and of divine restraint. The rage and fury of vile and vain passion, without the slightest restriction from God, will doubtless afford a considerable portion of the torments of hell, joined to the undying worm of a polluted and awakened conscience. Now, from these last sources of anguish, it is manifest that the Saviour must have been exempt. He, therefore, could not have endured the full amount of misery due to the sins of all mankind, because he never could have forfeited the sanctifying influences of the blessed Spirit, nor have become subject to the distressing consciousness of heinous personal guilt.

Yet was the suffering of Christ not the less vicarious upon this account. It was in our stead as fully as if it had been our actual punishment; for the term "vicarious" does not necessarily imply the performance or the endurance, by a substitute, of all that would otherwise have been performed or endured, but merely that sort of substitution which, to all practical purposes, shall be sufficient to exonerate another: and that the suffering of Christ was vicarious to this extent, I have already endeavoured to show. Still less does this view detract from the value of the atonement, since that was determined by other causes. The union of the Godhead with his humanity gave an infinite dignity to all he did, and rendered his sufferings, in the abstract, worthy of all reverence and consideration. Their absolute spontaneity gave them the highest conceivable legal value; while the glory which they reflected upon the person and government of God, with their practical results, rendered them, in a moral sense, infinitely meritorious and available. These considerations appear to render needless any further suffering than what is absolutely involved in them; and that, it is unnecessary to add, was deep and dreadful beyond mental conception.

I have gone into this somewhat extended discussion, to show, as you will probably have anticipated, that, even according to our notions of justice, there is no obstacle to the affixing of certain conditions to a personal participation of the results of Christ's vicarious sacrifice. Of course, the converse is equally certain, that the calamities which await those who finally reject these conditions are in the highest degree justifiable. But it is necessary to add even more than this; for we are incapable of conceiving of the atonement as producing that amplitude of moral good of which it may be rendered the source, by an unconditional application of the pardon which it provides. If this were granted universally, it is plain, that the moral government of God would, to all practical purposes, be terminated among men; while, if it were applied arbitrarily, it would be productive of consequences scarcely less deplorable. I presume, I need not pause to make out this position, as it will at once commend itself to your own mind. It follows, therefore, that the deliverance from condemnation, which is the most obvious of the blessings resulting from the atonement, does, by the divine appointment, depend upon certain conditions which are unchangeable in their nature, and indissoluble in their obligation.

If the existence of these conditions be allowed, it will, I suppose, be conceded also, that they must, in their nature, be in perfect harmony with the general scheme of the atonement, and must be most perfectly suited to accomplish its objects. Now, though the first design of the vicarious suffering of Christ which attracts attention is a deliverance from the curse of the law, because it is primarily a judicial arrangement, yet it is never to be forgotten, that it has for its further and more exalted object, the restoration of man to the possession of that resemblance to his Creator by which he was originally distinguished; an object to which, in fact, the former and more obvious does but lead the way. When, therefore, I speak, as hereafter I shall have occasion to do, of the blessings of the atonement in general, or of salvation in an indefinite sense, I beg to be understood as including not merely the removal of guilt, but that great spiritual process also which, by the sacred writers, is called "sanctification," &c.

With these preliminary remarks on this part of the subject I must, at present, content myself. In my next letter I propose to speak more at large of the conditions upon which the benefits of the vicarious sacrifice of Christ are made to depend.

Letter XV.

My dear Friend,

In my last letter I endeavoured to show that it was not only righteous, but even necessary, for God to associate the benefits of Christ's atonement with certain conditions; and this leads us to the consideration of the fifth and last requisite for a just and available vicarious sacrifice, which is,—that the offenders shall accept it upon the terms proposed by the other parties to such an arrangement. It is so evident that God and Christ are alone able to determine upon what conditions it will be proper to admit sinners to a participation of the blessings resulting from the Gospel scheme of substitution, that every degree of latitudinarianism upon the subject may naturally awaken our surprise. For, although when God reveals to us his method of saving men through Christ, we may immediately perceive its reasonableness; yet, were this not the fact, the most perfect acquiescence upon our part would still be our duty and our wisdom. For he has the plan of mercy all in his own hands; and it is for him, therefore, to arrange all its details absolutely and without change. In its origination and its provisions we had no share, and in the nature of things could have none. God's grace is its fountain; and, apart from our approbation, therefore, he has the most perfect right to determine all its operations. His character gives us every assurance that he will do that which is righteous and wise; and our weakness of understanding and obliquity of judgment would be sufficient to account for any want of apprehension as to the propriety of his principles of government. Can anything, therefore, be more arrogant than for a human mind to rise up in judgment upon the divine testimony respecting the salvation of sinners in Christ? to attempt to remodel the plan which God has given? to speak peace to him to whom God has not spoken peace? or to defy him whom God hath not defied? Yet this is, in fact, the conduct of those who deviate in the smallest degree from the statements of the Bible upon this subject, and who give an unscriptural latitude or restriction to the conditions upon which God promises to receive sinful man to his grace and salvation. You will at once discern, that we cannot be too inflexible in our adherence to the simple statement of Scripture; and that the smallest departure from it leads us into serious, if not fatal, error.

I need not tell you, that the testimony of the Bible upon this subject is most clear and decisive: "He that believeth shall be saved." And this, as you well know, is repeated in various forms of expression throughout the word of God. Suffer me, then, to bring before you, as briefly as may be, the several acts which may scripturally be supposed to be implied in believing, or to be necessarily connected with it; and while I go through this detail, you will, I think, be able to perceive how admirably such a condition of salvation is suited at once to the character of God, and to the condition of the sinner.

The first and most obvious sense of the term is, the intellectual apprehension and admission of those truths which are accompanied by a sufficient degree of moral evidence; which evidence, nevertheless, falls short of absolute certainty. "Faith," in this sense, as well as others, "cometh by hearing, and hearing by the word of God." This definition of faith will not, I suppose, be disputed by any; and from it, it follows, that, supposing the opportunities of men to be sufficient, there is no salvation for those who do not admit certain doctrines to be true and divine. You will also clearly see, that the object of saving faith, in this and every other acceptation of the term, is Jesus Christ. "Believe on the Lord Jesus Christ, and thou shalt be saved," is the tenor of the canon. There may be some varieties in the views of men respecting Christ; but it is undeniable, that there are fundamental truths which regard his person and work which are essential to salvation. His divinity is certainly one of these; for if Christ be really and essentially God, he who represents him as anything short of that character does him infinite wrong, and can more be said to exercise faith in him than in Moses or St. Paul. For, the distinction between creatures is, after all, inconsiderable; and Christ, if, according to the Arian hypothesis, he be only a super-angelic creature, is infinitely remoter from God than the meanest reptile is from him. The Infinite is infinite in every sense, and in reference to every measure; and however exalted any finite being may be, the Infinite is beyond him still, and unchangeably infinite. I repeat it, therefore, —every opinion which deprives Christ of his Godhead, is a fatal heresy. This, I say, without pausing to adduce proof of what I have already argued,—the real and proper divinity of our Lord.

The doctrine of the atonement is another of those fundamental truths upon which correct apprehensions are necessary to salvation. For if God has appointed us to be saved by faith in the vicarious sacrifice of Christ, it is manifest that a rejection of it is, in effect, a rejection of salvation. Otherwise, that sacrifice is needless. If man can be saved by other means, God's gift of his Son is mere prodigality; which is too impious a conclusion to be allowed for one moment. I shall not stop to prove that the vicarious sacrifice of Christ is essential to our salvation, as upon that topic I have before descanted. Taking this for granted, then, our position is, that there is no salvation except through an admission of this truth; supposing, of course, that opportunities are afforded for being instructed in its nature and evidences.

Still further: we contend, that in this arrangement there is no harshness; but that it is in every respect suitable to the Creator and his creatures. Are we reminded of human imbecility, and the dimness of the mind of man, as an apology for his unbelief? No resource surely can be more inappropriate. For what is the tone assumed by the rejecters of these doctrines? Are they indeed spirits oppressed with a sense of intellectual infirmity? Are there complaints continually of the inadequacy of their faculties to the apprehension of divine truth? Do they bow their heads before God, overwhelmed with servile and stupid dread, deeming his mysteries a great deep which cannot be fathomed? No: they are "as gods, knowing good and evil;" they are, *par excellence*, rational beings: this is their pride, their boast, their distinction. Their rejection of the doctrines of the Bible is, because they are too wise, too perfectly cultivated, to submit to them. The testimony of God is foolishness to such spirits. They carry their objections to the throne of their Creator, and esteem themselves perfectly competent to determine how he shall judge and govern. To the feeble and humble mind, the word of God is perfectly adapted. It supplies the truth in its simplest form, and all they have to do is to receive it,—a matter to them of no considerable difficulty. And if pride is not made for man; if it is a sin and a curse; if it dishonours God, and defiles the human soul; it is easy to perceive how proper it is to demand, in the first place, the submission and acquiescence of the understanding to truths which, on their very front, suggest to us our incapacity and weakness.

It is absurd to complain of severity in the divine demand upon our faith; because, the mere hesitation to admit any divinely-testified truth, is an evidence of a state of mind inconsistent with salvation, not from the appointment of God merely, but from the nature of things. For, if any individual rejects a scriptural doctrine, on the account of its not according with his own views and judgment, he is clearly in a condition of proud and presumptuous rebellion against the divine authority; and while he remains in that state of mind, his salvation involves a contradiction. He cannot be saved from sin, and yet continue in such a sin as his unbelief necessarily involves; or else he is saved and unsaved at the same moment. Now the first and lowest indication of a man's submitting himself to God is, the admission of the truth of what God has declared; and till this takes place, there is no more severity in saying that he cannot be saved, than there is in saying that a triangle cannot contain more than three angles, or that there cannot be perfect darkness and perfect light at one and the same instant.

There is further implied in that faith which brings salvation, an admission of the righteousness of the law of God. Hence the Apostle Paul, in describing an initial state of grace, says, "I consent unto the law, that it is good;" and he goes so far as to express the strength of the awakened sinner's approbation of it thus: "I delight in the law of God after the inward man,"—even that law by which he just before had declared that the sinner was judicially slain, and by which his sin was rendered peculiarly heinous in his own eyes. "What shall we say then? Is the law sin? God forbid. Nay, I had not known sin, but by the law: for I had not known lust, except the law had said, Thou shalt not covet. But sin, taking occasion by the commandment, wrought in me all manner of concupiscence. For without the law sin was dead. For I was alive without the law once: but when the commandment came, sin revived, and I died. And the commandment, which was ordained to life, I found to be unto death. For sin, taking occasion by the commandment, deceived me, and by it slew me. Wherefore the law is holy, and the commandment holy, and just, and good. Was then that which is good made death unto me? God forbid. But sin, that it might appear sin, working death in me by that which is good; that sin by the commandment might become exceeding sinful. For we know that the law is spiritual: but I am carnal, sold under sin. For that which I do I allow not: for what I would, that do I not; but what I hate, that do I. If then I do that which I would not, I consent unto the law that it is good. Now then it is no more I that do it, but sin that dwelleth in me. For I know that in me (that is, in my flesh) dwelleth no good thing: for to will is present with me; but how to perform that which is good I find not. For the good that I would I do not: but the evil which I would not, that I do. Now if I do that I would not, it is no more I that do it, but sin that dwelleth in me. I find then a law, that, when I would do good, evil is present with me. For I delight in the law of God after the inward man: but I see another law in my members, warring against the law of my mind, and bringing me into captivity to the law of sin which is in my members. O wretched man that I am! who shall deliver me from the body of this death? I thank God through Christ Jesus our Lord. So then with the mind I myself serve the law of God; but with the flesh the law of sin." (Rom. vii. 7-25.)

These passages describe the state of mind which, though not in the actual exercise of faith, is undergoing the discipline necessary to its existence. This, you will perceive, is what is elsewhere called "repentance;" a godly sorrow, wrought in the heart by the blessed Spirit, resulting from a sense of the holiness of the law, and of repeated and inexcusable violations of it, and accompanied by an approbation of its righteous demands, an admission of the justness of its penalties, and an earnest endeavour to abandon those evils which ensure its curse. This is not faith, nor does it constitute any part of faith; but it necessarily precedes it; as the same Apostle teaches us: "The law is our schoolmaster to bring us to Christ, that we might be justified by faith." (Gal. iii. 24.) Need I pause to remark on the suitableness of this disposition to our condition as sinners, and its appropriateness as introductory to the great doctrine of the atonement? I may just remark, that, as before the mercy of God could be shown to man, his justice was to be vindicated, so, in harmony with this procedure, before salvation can be conveyed to an individual, it is in the highest degree fitting that he should feel something of that condemnation under which the law places him; and that, not merely because of the moral benefit involved in such a process, but in order that thus the provisions of the Gospel may, in some degree, be the subject of suitable estimation.

Closely allied to this, and inseparably connected with it in the progress of a man towards the actual exertion of faith, is a spirit of entire self-renunciation. For it is worthy of notice, that a sense of the condemnation of the law, and of our inability to fulfil its requisitions, is not immediately accompanied with a consciousness that we are incapable of doing any single act to obtain the favour of God. For when a sinner is compelled to abandon all hope from the naked law, he is yet disposed to seek for salvation through a certain legalized form of the Gospel.

To his penitence or his prayers, he, in a measure, trusts for receiving that pardon which Christ has procured. For though he admits that salvation results wholly from the atonement, he still cherishes the hope that, by reformation and general moral improvement, he may, in some degree, qualify himself to claim the blessings which are purely of grace. But, however good and proper repentance and amendment of life may be and actually are, it is never to be forgotten that they supply no sort of right to the salvation of Christ. Nothing is to interfere with his merit, nothing to neutralize the value of his sufferings. And the divine jealousy upon this subject is as beneficial to man as it is honourable to God. It is a part of Christ's reward, not only that men shall be saved by him, but that they shall be indebted to him alone for salvation. Nor can that man be said to be in a proper state of mind to enjoy and to value a state of pardon, who is not disposed in the most unreserved way to ascribe all that he possesses to the free and pure mercy of God in Christ. Any feeling short of this implies an imperfect conception of the prevalence of the atonement; and the happiness, prosperity, and security of the Christian depends, in a great degree, upon the clearness and amplitude of his views upon this subject. Thus, therefore, does God, for his own glory, and for the real and permanent good of the sinner himself, require that he should renounce every description of trust in his own powers or morality, and submit himself under a sense of utter destitution to the divine provision for his emergencies.

That act of faith by which a sinner obtains justification results immediately from a firm persuasion of the value and prevalency of the atonement; and consists of an unreserved acceptance of it, and an implicit reliance upon it, as a divinely appointed means for salvation. He who thus trusts in Christ is, in the New-Testament sense, a believer; while he who neglects or refuses to do so is an unbeliever. Hence the Apostle Paul employed the word "trust" as synonymous with belief, and thus describes the process of salvation in the case of the Ephesian Christians: "That we should be to the praise of his glory, who first trusted in Christ. In whom ye also trusted, after that ye heard the word of truth, the Gospel of your salvation: in whom also after that ye believed, ye were sealed with that holy Spirit of promise, which is the earnest of our inheritance until the redemption of the purchased possession, unto the praise of his glory." (Ephes. i. 12-14.) I need not tell you how frequently the same view is to be found in the Old Testament, where trust in God is represented as the source of all blessedness and security. Consider, then, in how admirable harmony with the scheme of the atonement, and how eminently suitable to the relations of man to his Creator, is such a condition of salvation. For you will observe, that there are necessarily involved in it peculiarly comprehensive and impressive views of the divine character, as exhibited in the work of Christ; and while these are in themselves very honourable to God, they are also, in no small degree, of moral benefit to man. This the apprehension of truth is in all cases, so far as its influence is practical; and the faith of the Gospel is distinguished by its energy in determining human conduct. The confidence in question cannot exist without a degree of love to God, as well as perception of his goodness; and in its further operation, it not only strengthens this principle, but gives it a mighty power over all the faculties of the spirit. It is the strongest moral motive of which man is capable, and leads to diligent obedience, to patient endurance, to universal benevolence, And this, it is to be recollected, is the result of scriptural affiance in God through Christ, not merely because God has ordained that it should be so, but in its own natural operation. For a sense of the amazing extent of the divine love, duly impressed upon the mind, must, in the nature of things, produce a reciprocation of love; and such a perception of the subject is necessary to that trust which we are now considering. Any degree of apprehension of evangelical truth insufficient to induce trust in God's mercy through Christ, is incapable of generating the love of the Gospel If there be not love, there is not a fulfilment of that law which belongs to the dispensation under which we live; for all the law is fulfilled in this one word. That the righteousness of this law might be fulfilled in us, was the reason of God's sending his Son. God's design in the atonement, therefore, can only be accomplished by the production of love to him in our hearts. And as this love cannot exist in the absence of faith, so in the absence of faith man cannot be saved.

And besides that salvation is, in the nature of things, impossible except by faith, God, to render the subject the more impressive, has represented unbelief as the greatest possible insult and wrong to himself. "Him that honoureth me," is his declaration, "I will honour." He that receives Christ, receives him that sent Christ: "And he that honoureth me," says Christ, "him will my Father honour." Nothing, certainly, can be more just than such an arrangement. But "he that believeth not hath made God a liar;" and surely such a spirit ought to be rejected by God, and cut off from the provisions which he has made. To doubt the fidelity of an upright man, when he has given every possible assurance of the truth of his representations, is certainly very discreditable; but to refuse our confidence to the God of truth, whose love has been manifested by the greatest possible condescension, and whose promises are accumulated throughout the Bible almost beyond calculation, is an impiety so great as to render the punishment of the unbeliever matter of imperative necessity. No such outrage of the divine rights could be tolerated without the most palpable dishonour to God's government. All complaints of harshness or severity in the terms of Gospel salvation are utterly pointless; since it is impossible to conceive of any sin more perfectly subversive of the divine authority than unbelief, nor of any condition of salvation more honourable to God, or morally beneficial to man, than faith.

I HAVE NOW, my dear friend, completed my remarks upon the harmony of the doctrine of the atonement in itself, and have brought before you what, to my own mind, are the most forcible illustrations of its fitness. I am not conscious of having made any representations to you but what are capable of the most substantial proof. In the course of my reflections upon the various subjects which I have brought before you, I have had occasion to abandon several opinions which I before entertained, and to modify certain others; but the more the great subject under consideration has opened to my mind, and the more deeply I have studied the train of argument pursued, the more fully have I been convinced of the truth of the doctrine, and of the abundant evidence with which it is accompanied. That the same effect should at once be produced upon your mind, is perhaps too much to be reasonably hoped for; but before I dismiss this part of the subject, I must take the opportunity of reminding you of the peculiar force possessed by reasoning of the sort to which, in my recent letters, I have directed your attention. It may be laid down as a demonstrable rule, that truth is invariably harmonious, and falsehood as regularly discordant. In fact, it is by this rule that the one is distinguished from the other; and there is no system nor single opinion which we do not test by it. But it is to be recollected, that internal harmony, though not so striking an evidence of truth, is nevertheless its invariable characteristic; and that every system is rationally decided upon to be true upon this ground alone, if there be no reason for discrediting its external evidence. Now, in the case before us, it is plain that the vicarious sacrifice of Christ is declared in the most unequivocal terms in the Bible, and that nothing but an exceedingly irrational and disingenuous mode of interpretation can get rid of the force of such declarations. If this doctrine be true, it is difficult to conjecture in what way the sacred writers could have expressed themselves to satisfy us upon the subject, if we are not satisfied by what they have actually stated. There is no ground, therefore, for questioning the doctrine from an insufficiency of external evidence. If, then, it be internally harmonious, it cannot be otherwise than true.

Yet I must not fail to remind you of the comprehensiveness of the harmony which I have brought before you. It is the concord of all that we know of God, of Christ, and of ourselves, and equally of all that we can rationally and scripturally conjecture of the inhabitants of the universe, from the meanest of men, to "the rapt seraph that adores and burns." Let me then propose it to your common sense, Is it possible that all this should be admitted, and yet that the doctrine in question should be false? If it be, who was its inventor? Whose was the mighty mind that concocted and arranged a system of error so beautiful, so harmonious, so attractive? Where did it originate, and under what circumstances? I confess, I am utterly at a loss to conjecture the era to which it will be ascribed; for I know no period of the church in which it did not exist, nor can I conceive that it is possible for it to take a later date than the age of Christ and his Apostles. And this is sufficient to content me. With them I am satisfied to be in truth or in error. I have no higher ambition than that my soul should be gathered with theirs, and that God should give me to share their portion. Nor will you, I am persuaded, dissent from me. Go, then, to the inquiry, as to the period in which the doctrine of the atonement was originated; and if you find no possibility of giving it any later era than that in which Jesus suffered, and Paul preached, you need not be afraid to admit its truth, and to be the companion of the goodly fellowship of the Apostles in the kingdom and patience of Jesus.

It may, however, be suggested to you, that the only direct scriptural proof which I have hitherto advanced has been that of isolated passages. Before I close our correspondence, therefore, I will take occasion to inquire how far the doctrine of the atonement harmonizes with the general tenor of Scripture; and this I will endeavour to do in my next letter.

Letter XVI.

My dear Friend,

It is to me a satisfaction that you admit my argument to possess any degree of cogency, and that you are interested in its prosecution. According to your wishes and my own proposal, I now offer to your consideration a few suggestions upon the general harmony of Scripture with those views of the atonement which I have already brought before you. The institutes of Moses have been adverted to. These supply not harmony merely, but analogy, both illustrative and confirmatory. Their prominence in the records of the Old Testament renders it needless that I should refer with any particularity to that part of holy Scripture. The succeeding remarks, therefore, you will understand to belong principally to the New Testament.

It is, I suppose, generally possible for an attentive mind, after having gone through any book, so far to abstract itself from mere details, as to realize a distinct impression from the whole. The difference between the spectator of a fair landscape, and a person in such circumstances, seems to be, that, in the one case, the perception of the whole precedes the examination of its parts, while in the other, the aggregate character is apprehended by a previous progression through details. This difference is easily accounted for; but there is little doubt that the perception of the lovely, or of the grand, may be as vivid from that which is intellectual, as from that which is sensible. Now, let me inquire what is the impression made upon your mind by the perusal of the New Testament. Abstract yourself as much as possible from its history and doctrine; and ascertain, as distinctly as may be, what, on the whole, is the character of your perceptions. You are at a loss to express them; and I am disposed to think, that, to a philosophic mind, endowed with any considerable degree of sensibility, there is always, under the same circumstances, a similar difficulty. Yet you are conscious of something extraordinary, magnificent, superhuman, in what has been brought before you. You may be unable, at the moment, to place your hand on the particular fact which has produced the impression; you may be unable to single out any passage which has struck you as at all adequate to the production of your actual emotions; but, on the whole, you have no difficulty in pronouncing, that you have been beyond the range of this visible and diurnal sphere, and that you have conversed with things divine. Rousseau, a judge on such a subject of a very high order, has recorded his emotions in the following celebrated passage:— "I will confess to you, that the majesty of the Scriptures strikes me with admiration, as the purity of the Gospel has its influence on my heart. Peruse the works of our philosophers, with all their pomp of diction: how mean, how contemptible, are they, compared with the Scriptures! Is it possible that a book, at once so simple and sublime, should be merely the work of man? Is it possible that the sacred Personage, whose history it contains, should be himself a mere man? Do we find that he assumed the tone of an enthusiast or ambitious sectary? What sweetness, what purity in his manners! What an affecting gracefulness in his delivery! What sublimity in his maxims! What profound wisdom in his discourses! What presence of mind in his replies! How great the command over his passions! Where is the man, where the philosopher, who could so live and so die, without weakness and without ostentation? — When Plato described his imaginary good man with all the shame of guilt, yet meriting the highest rewards of virtue, he described exactly the character of Jesus Christ: the resemblance was so striking that all the Christian Fathers perceived it.

"What prepossession, what blindness must it be, to compare the son of Sophronicus [Socrates] to the Son of Mary! What an infinite disproportion is there between them! Socrates, dying without pain or ignominy, easily supported his character to the last: and if his death, however easy, had not crowned his life, it might have been doubted whether Socrates, with all his wisdom, was anything more than a vain sophist. He invented, it is said, the theory of morals. Others, however, had before put them in practice: he had only to say, therefore, what they had done, and to reduce their examples to precept. — But where could Jesus learn among his competitors that pure and sublime morality of which he only has given us both precept and example? The death of Socrates peaceably philosophizing with his friends, appears the most agreeable that could be wished for; that of Jesus, expiring in the midst of agonizing pains, abused, insulted, and accused by a whole nation, is the most horrible that could be feared. Socrates, in receiving the cup of poison, blessed the weeping executioner, who administered it; but Jesus, in the midst of excruciating tortures, prayed for his merciless tormentors. Yes! if the life and death of Socrates were those of a sage, the life and death of Jesus were those of a God. Shall we suppose the evangelic history a mere fiction? Indeed, my friend, it bears not the marks of fiction: on the contrary, the history of Socrates, which nobody presumes to doubt, is not so well attested as that of Jesus Christ. Such a supposition, in fact, only shifts the difficulty, without obviating it: it is more inconceivable that a number of persons should agree to write such a history, than that one only should furnish the subject of it. The Jewish authors were incapable of the diction, and strangers to the morality, contained in the Gospel; the marks of whose truth are so striking and inimitable, that the inventor would be a more astonishing man than the hero." This passage it is almost impossible to read without consentaneous emotion.

Now, the question simply is, Are these perceptions or impressions true or false? Is it a fact, that the New Testament is a record of this extraordinary character? Is its whole train of history and doctrine really calculated to waken our surprise, and to impress us with the consciousness of this unparalleled sublimity? or are our emotions altogether factitious? I say, that this is the simple question that awaits our decision; for put out of the New Testament the doctrine of the atonement, and the other truths inseparably associated with it, and it is demonstrable that all such notions are extravagant and visionary. For what is a system of morals, however pure; and what the history of a few martyrs, however distinguished; but the representation of truth with which, in one degree or other, we are perfectly familiar? The doctrine of man's immortality possesses no such power to elevate, embarrass, and even oppress.

We know that we are immortal: our certainty upon the subject, it is true, is attained through the revelations of the New Testament; but they, after all, merely carry out into assurance the suggestions of our own minds.

MEMBERS OF SCHMUL'S WESLEYAN BOOK CLUB
BUY THESE OUTSTANDING BOOKS AT 40% OFF
THE RETAIL PRICE

Join Schmul's Wesleyan Book Club by calling toll-free:
$$800\text{-}S_7P_7B_2O_6O_6K_5S_7$$

Put a discount Christian bookstore in your
own mailbox

Visit us on the Internet at
www.wesleyanbooks.com

Schmul Publishing Company | PO Box 776 | Nicholasville, KY 40340

www.ingramcontent.com/pod-product-compliance
Lightning Source LLC
LaVergne TN
LVHW051521070426
835507LV00023B/3226